AN OLD WOMAN'S REFLECTIONS

The Blasket Islands are three miles off Ireland's Dingle Peninsula. Until their evacuation just after the Second World War, the lives of the 150 or so Blasket Islanders had remained unchanged for centuries. A rich oral tradition of story-telling, poetry, and folktales kept alive the legends and history of the islands, and has made their literature famous throughout the world. The seven Blasket Island books published by Oxford University Press contain memoirs and reminiscences from within this literary tradition, evoking a way of life which has now vanished.

The Western Island
Robin Flower

A Pity Youth Does Not Last
Mícheál O'Guiheen

A Day in Our Life
Seán O'Crohan

Twenty Years A-Growing
Maurice O'Sullivan

The Islandman
Tomás O'Crohan

An Old Woman's Reflections
Peig Sayers

Island Cross-Talk
Tomás O'Crohan

PEIG SAYERS

An Old Woman's
Reflections

Translated from the Irish by
SÉAMUS ENNIS
and introduced by
W. R. RODGERS

OXFORD
UNIVERSITY PRESS

OXFORD
UNIVERSITY PRESS

Great Clarendon Street, Oxford OX2 6DP

Oxford University Press is a department of the University of Oxford.
It furthers the University's objective of excellence in research, scholarship,
and education by publishing worldwide in

Oxford New York

Athens Auckland Bangkok Bogotá Buenos Aires Calcutta
Cape Town Chennai Dar es Salaam Delhi Florence Hong Kong Istanbul
Karachi Kuala Lumpur Madrid Melbourne Mexico City Mumbai
Nairobi Paris São Paulo Singapore Taipei Tokyo Toronto Warsaw

with associated companies in Berlin Ibadan

Oxford is a registered trade mark of Oxford University Press
in the UK and in certain other countries

First published 1962
Reissued 2000

Acknowledgements are due to the Department of Education, Irish Publications Branch, Dublin,
and to Miss Mary Kennedy for permission to publish this translation of
Machtnamh Sena Mhná by Peig Sayers, edited by Mary Kennedy, Dublin, 1939;
to Mr Mícheál Ó'Gaoithin, to whom his mother originally dictated these reminiscences;
and also to Jonathan Cape Ltd, for permission to quote the lines from *The Silver Branch*
by Séan O'Faoláin on p. xii.

British Library Cataloguing in Publication Data

Data available

Library of Congress Cataloging in Publication Data
Sayers, Peig.
[Machtnamh sena mhná. English]
An old woman's reflections—Peig Sayers ; translated from the
Irish by Séamus Ennis and introduced by W.R. Rodgers.
p. cm.
Originally published: London ; New York ; Oxford University Press, 1962.
1. Blasket Islands (Ireland)—Social life and customs. 2. Sayers,
Peig—Homes and haunts—Ireland—Blasket Islands. 3. Blasket
Islands (Ireland)—Biography. I. Title.
DA990.B65S33 1993 941.9'6—dc20 93-31555

ISBN-13: 978-0-19-281239-1

29

Printed in Great Britain by
Clays Ltd, St Ives plc

Contents

PEIG

By courtesy of Tomás Ó Muircheartaigh

Introduction

The day's dusty duty has been done, the last boat drawn up on the strand, and the mountain-sides and sea-lochs that fringe the western coast of Ireland are dark. But in a white-washed kitchen in the glen the peat-fire glows like a berry, and the cricket—'the cock of the ashes'—sings. And the tangle of Gaelic voices singles out as the Story-teller spreads his fingers for attention and begins his tale. It could well be a wonder-tale that crossed the roads of Europe from the East a thousand years ago; passing from mouth to mouth and from generation to generation till at last it comes to rest in this lamp-lit room at the edge of the Atlantic. For an hour or two the listening farmers and fisher-men will forget their bleak existence; the intoxicating talk turns them into kings and playboys of the western world. 'And tell me,' said a Kerryman, 'if you had no picture-house, no playhouse, no cunning radio or television at the tips of your fingers, no amusement whatever from head to head of the week except what was painted on the square above a cottage half-door (the highest excitement being the coming and going of cloud-caps on a mountain) wouldn't you too be hungry for the lovely dovetailed talk?'

The Gaelic story-tellers are the caretakers of a peasant tradition, the carriers of an oral culture, that once covered the Atlantic fringe of Europe. They belong to antiquity, to a Europe that had no books, no radio, no cinema or tele-vision, a Europe whose only entertainment was the parish lore or the winter-night's tale told by a passing traveller. Unlettered but not unlearned, they are the inheritors of a considerable art. Usually they are old men, for it is the old who think long and sleep lightly and have the fabulous memories. But the story-tellers are a vanishing race for they have lost their audience and the flow of words comes thin and seldom now. The radio has taken away their voices just as the printed page has taken over their memories, and the pictures that once were seen in a glowing peat-fire are seen more readily on the picture-screen today. The world has widened and the imagination of man has dwindled. For it is *good* communications, not evil ones, that corrupt good manners and local *mores*, and the better the roads that lead into the glen the quicker the old language, the old customs, the old stories and poetry, run out of it. I recall going to visit a Gaelic story-teller who was reputed to be the only man left in his district who could tell in the traditional manner *The King of Ireland's Son*, a tale that took him two weeks of nights in the telling. He was not at home; I found him in his enemy's house, the local cinema, watching a Wild Western picture.

'Those old story-tellers had extraordinary memories,' said an elderly schoolmaster to me. 'They could remember a story, even if it were as long as a book, after hearing it once. That was the important thing, for they could neither read nor write. There was one particular house for story-telling in our district and my father went every second night and myself along with him. We had a great respect for emulation then. I was fifteen at the time, and whether in Gaelic or English I'd be delighted with the fairy-stories. Going home at night I'd be thinking of them, and if a widowed leaf dropped from a holly-bush I'd leap a foot with the fright. But the young people are not interested now.' Fairy tales, ghost stories, and similar short narrative pieces (*seanchas*[1])

---

[1] *Seanchaí* is applied as a rule to a person, man or woman, who makes a speciality of local tales, family sagas or genealogies, social-historical tradition and the like, and can recount many tales of a short realistic type about fairies, ghosts, and other supernatural beings (J. H. Delargy).

are recounted by both men and women. But the telling of the great Finn-tales (*fianaíocht*) or hero-stories is traditionally restricted to men; 'A woman *fianaí* or a crowing hen!' runs the proverb. And the long and popular folk-tales (*sean-sgéalta*) are also mainly preserved by men. There have been notable exceptions to this rule. From Peig Sayers, 'the Queen of Gaelic story-tellers', one collector, Seósamh Ó Dálaigh, obtained 375 tales, of which forty were long folk-tales: forty folk-songs were also taken down from her dictation.

Peig Sayers (1873–1958), was born in the parish of Dunquin at the western end of the Dingle peninsula in the county of Kerry. In Kerry they say that the gift of poetry passes from father to daughter, the gift of story from father to son. But Peig, like her brothers, Pádraig and Seán, had the stories from her father, 'and I don't think', she said to me,

that his master in story-telling was in Kerry at the time. It was a great pity that these gadgets and horns and machines weren't there then to take down his speech and conversation, but alas! they weren't. I remember well the night he was telling the story of *The Red Ox*. He was ninety-eight years old that night but was very lively and healthy. While he was at the story, telling it to us at the fireside, he stopped in the middle of it and wasn't able to say another word for a while.

'You're near death, father,' said I.

'I'm not,' said he.

'Indeed you are,' I replied. 'Death is coming for you. You never went astray in a story, as long as there's memory in my head, until tonight. You're finished!'

'Death hasn't left Cork yet to come for me, my girl!' said he. But it had. For he wasn't able to finish out the end of the story, and he lived only nine days after that. He had done a good deal to entertain the young boys—and the old too—who gathered round him to hear him. That was the chief pastime then, story-telling and talking about old times. But that's not the way now. They no longer care for stories, and the stories would have died out altogether, for the young people weren't ready to pick them up. But now, thank God, there's a gadget for taking them down, if there were any story-tellers left, but there aren't. For the old Gaels are dead and the new generations rising up don't know Irish well. That's a great pity because Irish is a noble and a precious language. But it is coming to life and regaining strength. And it is short, with God's help, until it will be blossoming again as it was in olden times by the old people who have left us. May God give eternal life to their souls and to our own souls when we seek it, Amen!

Peig married into a neighbouring island, the Great Blasket, where she spent the greater part of her life. 'I never met my husband till the day I married him,' she told me, 'but it was a love-match till the day he died. And why shouldn't it, for he was a fine big man.' Peig herself was a fine big woman. Peig Mhór (Big Peg) she was commonly called. 'Big Peig', wrote Robin Flower in his devoted book, *The Western Island*, 'is one of the finest speakers in the Island; she has so clean and finished a style of speech that you can follow all the nicest articulations of the language on her lips without any effort; she is a natural orator, with so keen a sense of the turn of phrase and the lifting rhythm appropriate to Irish that her words could be written down as they leave her lips, and they would have the effect of literature with no savour of the artificiality of composition.' Students and scholars of the Irish language came from far and wide to visit her and she received them with natural country dignity. 'I saw her being presented with a mushroom one day,' a neighbour told me, 'and she accepted it as if she had been presented with a gold cup.' Where life in general is limited and monotonous its least detail is exalted into drama; islanders who live in the shapeless shadow of poverty will always put a pattern of dignity and ceremony on it in order to endure and redeem their existence.

The Great Blasket Island lies three stormy miles from the mainland of Kerry. On this sea-birds' ledge of Europe, where the Atlantic waves rise up like swallows into the lofts of air, a hardy community of people kept a bare foothold for centuries. It was a slackening hold when I saw it fifteen years ago, for the island was plainly exhausted and the girls from the mainland would no longer marry into it; only fifty people were left on it. The few green fields ring-worming the rough hairy hillside, the old man holding on to the tail of his donkey as it climbed the mountainy path, the old woman hunkered at her cottage door, her face sunk in her hands, the absence of children playing, gave the place an air of approaching dereliction. Yet this small island had been a crowded nest of Gaelic life and story-telling, and had contributed several minor classics to the world of books: *The Islandman*, by Tomás Ó Crohan; *Twenty Years Agrowing*, by Maurice O'Sullivan; and now Peig's own *Reflections*. Seen on a summer's day from the cliff at Dunquin no prospect could be more pleasing: the sudden eye-openers of sunlight on the vast face of the Atlantic; the gannets flashing like far-off bits of mirror; the islands shading off as if shy of being seen; a perpetual flutter of wind, like paper tearing at one's ears. But in winter the Great Blasket is a bleak black place, and the islanders were often marooned by storm for three weeks at a time. The only access to the island at any time is by curragh, a fifteen-foot canoe (*naomhóg*) of lath and tarred canvas made for three rowers, with the ubiquitous sacred medal and bottle of holy water tied to the prow. Buoyant and biddable, it is the only boat that can live in these waters and land on this wild coast. But it is seldom that anyone lands on the Great Blasket now, for the island is quite deserted.

Remote in time as in space, these Gaelic-speaking regions

of the West have a medieval simplicity. The people are close to earth and to each other. Every field-stone has been hand-turned a thousand times and every turn of a man's mind is known. And Heaven, too, is close to earth here. It lies, explained an old Kerrywoman, in the south-west, 'a foot-and-a-half above the height of a man', as homely and intimate today as it was to the Gaelic poet of the Middle Ages:

> I would like to have the men of Heaven
> In my own house;
> With vats of good cheer
> Laid out for them.
>
> I would like to have the three Marys,
> Their fame is so great.
> I would like people
> From every corner of Heaven.
>
> I would like them to be cheerful
> In their drinking,
> I would like to have Jesus, too,
> Here amongst them.
>
> I would like a great lake of beer
> For the King of Kings.
> I would like to be watching Heaven's family
> Drinking it through all eternity.

'I wish I had the ability to describe the scene in Peig Sayers's home in Dunquin on a winter's night when the stage was set for the *seanchaí*', writes Seósamh Ó Dálaigh to me. 'The evening meal was over, the day's work done, the family rosary finished. On the hearth glowed a small peat-fire and on the side-wall an oil-lamp gave a dim light. Peig dominated the scene, seated on a low chair right in front of the fire (this was most unusual in the locality; *bean a' tí*, the woman of the house, usually seated herself at the side) and smoking her pipe. Mícheál her brother-in-law sat with his vamps[2] to the fire at one side of her and Mike her son at the other. When the visitors arrived (for all gathered to the Sayers house when Peig was there, to listen to her from supper-time till midnight) the chairs were moved back and the circle increased. News was swopped, and the news often gave the lead for the night's subject, death, fairies, weather, crops.' All was grist to the mill, the sayings of the dead and the doings of the living, and Peig, as she warmed to her subject, would illustrate it richly from her repertoire of verse, proverb, and story. Often her thoughts would turn to sad topics; she might tell, for instance, of the bitter day when the body of her son Tom was brought home, his head so battered by the cruel rocks he had fallen on from the cliff that his corpse was not presentable to the public. So Peig, with breaking heart, had gathered her courage together and with motherly hands had stroked and coaxed the damaged skull into shape. 'It was difficult,' she would say; and then, with a flick of the shawl she wore, she would invoke the name of the Blessed Virgin, saying 'Let everyone carry his cross.' 'I never heard anything so moving in my life,' a Kerryman confessed to me, 'as Peig Sayers reciting a lament of the Virgin Mary for her Son, her face and voice getting more and more sorrowful. I came out of the house and I didn't know where I was.' Great artist and wise woman that she was, Peig would at once switch from gravity to gaiety, for she was a light-hearted woman, and her changes of mood and face were like the changes of running water. As she talked her hands would be working too; a little clap of the palms to cap a phrase, a flash of the thumb over her shoulder to mark a mystery, a hand hushed to mouth for mischief or whispered secrecy. 'When the fun is at its height it is time to go', runs

2 Stockinged feet.

the Irish proverb; and when visitors went each night Peig would draw the ashes over the peat-embers to preserve the fire till morning, reciting her customary prayer: 'I preserve the fire as Christ preserves all. Brigid at the two ends of the house, and Mary in the centre. The three angels and the three apostles who are highest in the Kingdom of Grace, guarding this house and its contents until day.'

'It's hard to be growing old,' said Peig when I said good-bye to her in Dingle, 'but,' she added with a grin, 'I'll be talking after my death, my good gentleman.' So she will, for as the proverb says,

> *Is buaine port ná glór na n-éan*
> *Is buaine focal ná toice an tsael*

'A tune is more lasting than the song of the birds, and a word more lasting than the wealth of the world.'

W. R. RODGERS

CHAPTER ONE

A Pity how Youth goes

.My sorrow, isn't it many a twist life does! Isn't Youth fine!
—but alas! she cannot be held always! She slips away as
the water slips away from the sand of the shore. A person
falls into age unknown to himself. I think there are no two
jewels more valuable than Youth and Health. There's me
now, sat in a heap on a green sward beside the house,
reflecting and musing on the days of my youth. Och! wasn't
it I was agile and light then! Small thought I had that I'd
ever be a worn old one like this! On that fine harvest
evening long ago, coming from Dingle, when I sat on the
Jackdaw's Rock to rest and looking around me and west
at the islands, little did I think that 'twas on that Big
Island I'd have to spend my life! But, of course, if a person
knew, he could alter things, because I know now what hardship followed me. My sharp grief! it's too late today, but
thank God life is nearly spent for me, as over three score
years of it have gone by me and for not long more will I
be a safe mooring, hard as I may try.

I'm looking from me out on the sea, which is quiet and
shining. Many a tide went north and from the north in
eighteen years and forty since a boat from Dunquin was
drowned—be safe where it's told! Its memory is live in my
head, though I was only six years old that time. It was an
awful day. The morning was calm and the Dunquin people
decided to go to the Small Island to cut seaweed. There
wasn't a breeze from the sky and the sea was quite calm;
and a person would say it was far from treachery or damage.
There were eight men in each boat, strong courageous men.

My own father and my two brothers, Patrick and John, were in the boat *Tinte*,[1] may God have mercy on their souls! The three boats were floating at the Cliff of the Sticks when some thought came into the mind of Maurice Kane—he was the captain on the *Tinte*—and he wouldn't be pleased unless my brother John who was in the Ballinahow boat came with him. Because he was a tough hard man he'd rather have him in the boat than Mister Long. In that mind he put Mister Long out of the boat and took my brother, John, in his own boat with him. But that didn't stop Mister Long from going to cut seaweed that day. The poor man went in my brother's place in the other boat. Then the three boats were let out to sea together. When they reached the small island the people of the (big) island were there before them sharply cutting seaweed, a man with a knife, a man with a sickle, unclad save for flannel breeches. Every man was at his work and believe me a long time wasn't spent when the boats were full. When the tide turned to flow, and their boats full, the *Body*—that was the Ballinahow boat—was in the lead but when the tide strengthened, and the north-east wind, the water started to come into the boat because it was too full of seaweed. Then they started to throw the seaweed overboard. But my sharp grief! A rough tidal wave arose and ran in on them. The boat coming behind them on her course saw their drowning danger and started to throw their seaweed overboard quickly. It was the *Tinte* boat that caught them up first, the boat my father was in but alas! the *Body* was there before them, her keel upwards and all the crew drowned save one couple who managed to catch hold of the keel. They took the couple aboard and brought them to the Cliff of the Sticks. It was a sorrowful day because there wasn't a

[1] 'Maurice the Tent' was the captain's nickname because it was in a tent or cabin he lived.

man or a woman who would be able who wasn't heading for the harbour with the thousand cries of grief. I and other children were playing Blind Man's Buff when Kate, my brother's wife came, and she frightened.

'Take care of Paddy, asthoreen,' she said—that's the older son she had who was starting to walk.

'Where will yourself go?' said I.

'Musha, I don't know where I'll go now,' she said and she went from me, the old track west and fright in her. A woman and another woman followed after her.

When my mother rose out, because of not having good hearing, she didn't know what had happened.

'Where are those women to the west all going?' she said.

'God with us!' said Kate Jim—it was she answered—'The *Tinte* boat is drowned and Pat and John in under her.' The poor child didn't understand it and no less did she know which boat was drowned.

As soon as my mother heard that speech she let an awful cry out of her that could be heard equally well all over the parish. She couldn't go anywhere, but she went up on the top of the wall with every second cry for Pat and John. It wasn't my father she was lamenting, but her two sons. She wasn't long there, however, when she became dizzy and away with her across the wall in to a bush of briars and nettles. That's where the racket was! I had every screech about horror, unable to help her, but a woman I didn't know came, Kate Malone, who had come home from America a while before that. When she heard me screeching she came to where my mother had fallen, took her up gently and went on to give her back sense and reason. She told her it wasn't the *Tinte* boat that was drowned at all, but the Ballinahow boat and that Pat and John were safe.

And with that four came from west the big gate. 'O, Kate,' says she, 'there comes my Pat.'

She was right. He was there, surely, himself and John and my father and Owen Brown.

It was a sorrowful day in Dunquin. There were five widows and their orphans weeping bitterly.

CHAPTER TWO

St. Kathleen's Pilgrimage; an Old Woman from Ventry; and Other Matters

I am going back now on the little road of thoughts. A holiday in Ventry parish is St. Kathleen's day. Many people do the pilgrimage of the church in that blessed graveyard where the remains of Kathleen are buried, awaiting the resurrection. There is nobody who is to be buried in that graveyard who doesn't strive to make confession and receive Communion and hear Mass on the morning of that day, in honour of St. Kathleen.

Drawing on forty years ago, I was doing the pilgrimage. The memory of that day is still alive in my head. I see, I think, the crowds moving down the long road heading for the graveyard. Some of them were unwell but there was strong hope alight in their hearts that they would be well when returning, by the Grace of God and St. Kathleen. Among them was an aged old woman from Ventry parish, and we both laid into talk with each other. Many an interesting thing she told me about and it was I gave sharp ear to that old woman. She said she remembered a big bird in the likeness of a swan being seen on the gable of the church and that people were saying that it was St. Kathleen herself in the likeness of a swan was being seen there.

'Did you see her yourself?' said I.

'I saw her,' said she, 'over there in the window of the old chapel.'

'Was it day-time?' said I.

'It wasn't, asthore,' said she. 'We used to do the

pilgrimage long before day at that time. My mother was with me, may God have mercy on her soul, the poor woman.'

'It was the early rising that caused it and the imagination of the eyes,' said I, and I pretended to be very unbelieving altogether.

'No, my pet,' said she, 'because I'm not the first person ever to see her, but nobody saw her since the first "souper"[1] was sent to the graveyard.'

'I suppose,' said I again, moving her for talking, 'that you remember a lot?'

'Musha, my treasure,' said she, 'I used to, but I never had but a waxen head and any accuracy it ever had it is scarce now with it. The hardship of life did its share of the work. You've only to look at my forehead—the picture is there to be seen'—and she turned to me so suddenly that she startled me.

We were drawing nigh the graveyard by that time and the aged woman was very quiet. As soon as we got to the church gate I spoke to her, but she didn't answer me. 'Tis how she moved her head at me to let me know she was praying. When she had her prayer finished I told her to teach me that little prayer she was saying to herself.

'Yes,' she said, 'never go by a graveyard without saying it with a clean heart.'

'I will do my best,' said I, 'but say the words.'

'God salute you, O true ones of Christ who are lying in this graveyard awaiting resurrection! He who suffered death for your sake, may he give glorious resurrection to your souls!'

'Amen,' said I. 'That's a beautiful wish, O aged woman, and I have it now and I'll do my best to say it every time I pass a graveyard.'

[1] 'Souper'—the one who turned his religion for soup in the famine years.

'Do, my treasure,' said she, 'because soon we will all be in need of that wish. But you have the youth still, and long may you! Have you got the prayer they say in honour of Kathleen, the saint of the pilgrimage?'

'No,' I said, 'because there's neither prayer nor creed correct with the people now compared with those who were there in your youth.'

'Listen to me now,' said she, 'till I say it for you' and she started this way:

> May God and Mary salute you, St. Kathleen,
> And as they salute you I salute you.
> It's to you I came, complaining my pain
> And asking my cure in God's account
> God and Mary and you to ease it for me!

'By my hands, aged woman, that prayer is nice too and I'll treasure it to me.'

'Do,' said she, 'maybe the day would come yet when you might use it. Let us start now and do the pilgrimage in the name of God,' said she.

At that time there were many other people in small parties here and there about the graveyard, each with his rosary beads in hand praying fervently. There was none of them but had some relative stretched among the thousands in the graveyard and that made the praying far more sincere.

We started at the bottom of the graveyard and had to go around it ten times and say a decade of the Rosary on each round and then go on our knees at the Cross at the head of the graveyard and say five decades.

Myself and the old woman and two other women who were not too old were on our knees. I was watching the old woman keenly. Her two eyes were closed hard and the beads busy in her fingers and she praying. As soon as we were ready she stood up.

'Yes,' she said, 'we have that much done, thank God, and may it be for our good! But I am exhausted by the walking and the age.'

'You weren't like that one time, Kate,' said I.

'I wasn't, island-woman,' said she. 'It was I had the agility, though I can easily deny that today. A good run doesn't stay with the steed for ever. Don't you see that many a brave man and strong tough woman are stretched there on their backs growing grass, may God grant eternal rest to their souls!'

'Amen!' said I.

'Do you see that little tomb beside us?'

'I do,' said I.

'The one I'm going to talk about is lying quietly under that flagstone. When I look at the grave it makes me meditate. Isn't it funny with an old person who gets upset by small things! And the proverb didn't leave much out, because it says the old person is a child twice. It's well I knew the person who is asleep in it.'

'And who is he, Kate?' said I, eager to hear the story concerning him.

'Pats the Smith was his name,' said she, 'and 'tis how he was always a servant with a gentlewoman[2] living in Dingle. He was a small low-sized stocky lad with black hair and pale yellow complexion on him and for that reason not much sought by the love of young women. But the gentle-woman wanted to see him well settled, because he was in her service for long years. She herself was master of all the land from Barque Point to Slea Head. She had the Bay Farm under lease and often she spent some of her time there. She had boys and girls in her employ there and frequently many of them were not too grateful to her. She had another house in Glenfawn they called the Big House. She had

[2] Betty Rice—she is mentioned in *The Islandman*.

servants and workers there too. Pats the Smith was the principal at the Big House and it's under his hand everything was. The gentlewoman had great trust in him and a liking for him. She had planned to present the Big House and all the land that went with it to him if he would marry a young woman that she had chosen for him. But the young woman didn't like him at all. She scorned Pats the Smith and the Big House. Her nose would bleed if she met him! The women of the parish faulted him so why shouldn't she? He was yellow, he didn't walk nicely, he was stoop-shouldered—there was no fault in the world but he had. There was no good the gentlewoman being at her. If she were to present her whole estate she'd never give in to marry him.

'Shrove came. And the young woman's father wanted to make a match for her with another man. But when the gentlewoman heard that news she called to her a band of her own tenant men and told them what she had planned. There was no use in their refusing her because oppression was too strict on them. She told them to hide in some place and help Pats the Smith to abduct the young woman.

' "Herself and her father are gone to Dingle today making a match," she said, "and it's a bold deed for them to oppose me. But let it not go with them! Let me be obeyed. Let their step be watched, and we'll see that we'll win in the end," and she stood before them as straight as a soldier.

'The Saturday to come the young girl and her father and mother were in Dingle and myself and two other girls with them. My woe! It's little I expected the enemy was so near us. Ventry strand a lot of people used to go that time, because there was a short-cut there. It was the strand we took too coming home. Our enemy was in hiding at Bun an Teampaill awaiting us. Pats the Smith with a wild strong horse was a bit away from the rest. Nobody could see them because the night was too dark. As soon as we came to Bun an Teampaill the tail of the cart was suddenly leant upon and we were thrown out on the sand. No quicker that than two men tied up the young woman in the dark and carried her with them to where Pats the Smith was waiting and away with them for the Big House. I never saw a man without sense only Big John, the father, that night when he saw his daughter gone. It's not home he came but un-harnessed the horse, jumped on its back and away to the barrack. The police travelled at that time of the night tracing and searching for the young woman and they didn't leave high or low, a glen or hill or mountain until they came to the Big House. They saw a light there and made for it and 'tis how she was there before them.

' "Will you come home or will you stay there?" said the father to her.

' "I'll go home, without doubt," said she.

' "If you'd do what I say, young one," said the gentle-woman, for she was there too, "you'd stay where you are. There would be drink and music in your kitchen to the end-day of your life and no sweat on your brow. Go now and you'll regret it."

' "O gentlewoman," said she, "were you to give me the whole district I couldn't promise you that I'd marry Pats the Smith."

' "All good!" said the gentlewoman.

' "And will be bad!" said the girl's father, answering her out. "I must have satisfaction."

' "What satisfaction do you want?" said the gentle-woman.

' "I'll put to the law those who wronged me!" said he.

' "It's no good for you," said she.

' "I'll lose to the calf in the field with them," said he.

' "I'll lose to the shoe on my foot with them," said she, and she hit a kick on the ground. "Go now," said she, "and if he's to be without a wife for ever he won't have you."

'A little while after that Pats the Smith went to America. Shame wouldn't allow him to stay here because of this mistake. My poor fellow spent all his life working hard and when he came home his heart was broken and it wasn't long until he died. He's buried in that grave there, and the gentlewoman is in the grave nearest to him.'

'Is that the Rices' grave?' said I.

'It is, asthore,' said she. 'Though great to speak of awhile, there's none of their signs today but that flagstone you see on the grave. They and the Trents and the Fitzgeralds were the proudest and most spoken-of in west Kerry in their time. But not many of them lived after the foreigners' crooked treachery. 'Tis how Rice was hanged, the father of the gentlewoman, and his son. The foreign robbers gave the same treatment to the Trents, save for one youth of that noble family who succeeded in escaping on a race-horse his father had. The red army was after him. They came up with him at Ballymore. He was caught. The poor lad was in a fix, but the grey horse was good and he was a choice rider. The blood was noble—it stirred and flowed faster than usual. He turned his head backwards, on the grey mare's back—he had nothing to see but the foreign army.

' "Yes, little horse," said he, "our time is up, but my dependence on you today." And then he guided the grey horse towards the cliff. It wasn't a sulk the grey mare put up when she came to the edge of the cliff, but to carry her four hooves with her, clean over. When the foreign robbers came to the edge of the cliff they had to stop. Young Trent was gone on the grey mare and 'twas not known where he had faced. He never came back to this place and that place is called Trent's Jump[3] ever since.'

'I don't know, O aged woman, was he of the Fitzgeralds the man they used to call "the Brush"?' said I.

'Yes, surely,' said she, 'though it's a nickname. He was a musical courageous man. Robert Fitzgerald was his name and often he stood in the gap of danger among the men. He and six more of the lads were on the run and it happened that at that time someone related had a wedding and they made up their minds that they'd come to the wedding some time during the night. About midnight seven men strode the door into the wedding-house. Nobody recognized them because they were disguised but the man of the house had a suspicion they were Fenians, and welcomed them. He gave them food and drink and told them to have no fear, that his door was open to harvesters and that there was no crop he'd rather harvest than the one they were shaping. When they had enough to eat and drink Robert, "the Brush", spoke to the young woman:

' "If it would be your will to lead me to the table for a while?" said he.

' "It is, and welcome," said she.

' "Would it be your will to wet it and soap it?" said he. She looked at him, and all who were in looked at him.

' "You are drunk, good man," said she, "don't you see that table is as clean as a silken shirt?" and the red flush ran up in her fair cheek.

' "O daughter of my soul," said Robert, "it's not of cleanliness I speak. The whole world knows that you came of the most generous and clean-hearted stock in the district. But do as I say. It's unlikely I'll ask you again."

' "Do what he says!" said her father, angrily.

[3] An alternative telling of this story is in *Bealoideas*, vol. 1 (The Journal of the Irish Folklore Society).

'Then she got the soft water and soap.

' "Is that to your liking, good man?" said she and the blush going back bit by bit to where it was first. Robert rubbed his finger on it.

' "Length on your life!" said he, "it will do."

'He leaped up on the table and told a piper that was sitting in the corner to play "The Hard Summer" for him and he started dancing. There wasn't a gig out of anybody only looking at the dancer. When he had done that bout he leaped down from the table and stood on the door-flag and said:

> "I am the Sweep
> From the top of Martin Hill
> And where is the lad
> Who would use a board hard with me?"

'And away for ever with himself and his company.'

'Musha, I wonder was he caught up with?' said I.

'He wasn't,' said she. 'That treacherous enemy never caught him, though they were hard on his track. He succeeded in escaping to America.'

CHAPTER THREE

Red Tommy and Margaret O'Brien

O Eagle Mountain, isn't it the stately, noble shape you
have today on you! You are in the tied confusion of years,
but you show it not for your form is as pleasing as ever.
In the days of my childhood there was no other place under
the bright sun was brighter than you. You were but a
stone's throw from me then but the big watery sea is between you and me today. Wasn't it often Kate Jim and
myself up on your top hauling the turf! We were like two
hares that time. Your height would not trouble us. Oh! A
delight to my heart was the smell of your heather! Often
I'd pick a bunch of it and tie it into a fold of my dress. I'd
never tire of sniffing the scented smell up in my nose. But
now I've only the smell of the sea since I left you. It gives
me peace of mind to be looking at your brow without mist.
O king of a thousand powers, 'tis many a thought you
arouse in my heart. Am I not again a little girl, whilst I'm
looking over at you, going from bush to bush looking for
nests down along the riverside to the rapid of Coman's
Head! Kate Jim is with me again and we small, throwing
stones into the river and the current shooting them before
it like the bullet. A little bit up from us is Old William
taking his rest, his slane standing in the bog and he singing
Cait Ni Dhuibhir.[1] A bit above, there's a big cloud of smoke
going into the sky—it's people cutting turf and the hill on
fire around them. Down from us are the green fields of
Dunquin and lads and horses and ploughs harrowing and
tearing them. They are keen for the work.

[1] A patriotic song personifying Ireland as Kate O'Dwyer.

We are sitting near William where we have clear sight
of sea and land. The clean sky of spring is above us and
everyone's heart wide-open welcoming the soft, fresh spring.
William starts to talk:

'Musha my love God! What a gem Youth is! Every nice
thing is in her view. The difficulty of this world never
daunts her. She doesn't like to be under control—she likes
to be free, without tie, always. But isn't it quickly she goes!
Do ye see me today, children? I was once as airy as ye
but as the skull said to the army officer: "As you are today
I once was, and as I am today you will one day be." Ye
will too, if ye live for it.'

We had Youth ruling that day, but see how she slipped
by just as William that day said she would. You have the
same noble appearance but far from you am I and Kate Jim
and the people cutting turf. Far and away we are scattered,
some of us here and some of us there. Some of us are on
the Way of Truth,[2] and those of us who are not, small is
the strength or humour left with us. But God is good and
has a good Mother and He never failed the patient heart.

What's in my mind today, and I standing here, is Red
Thomas who was at Boundary, when he said great is the
value of patience. This Thomas was the son of a widow.
He was a quiet sensible good-looking boy but he had no
way of livelihood only his day's pay and seldom he had
even that at that time. Often a party of them would go
from Ventry parish and other places, digging potatoes north
beyond Tralee. Thomas's uncle was of one of these parties—
spalpeens they called them. Each man had his own spade
on his shoulder. There was a special place in Tralee which
was called Spalpeen Street, for they used all gather in that
street, and any farmer who wanted a pair or three could
find them in that street. Thomas's uncle and five other

[2] Gone to our Heavenly award.

spalpeens were in one house digging potatoes. The man of
the house was an independent farmer and a good man too.
He had no unmarried family save one daughter. The other
three were married out and every one of them well off.
Because he had no son it was to this woman he had planned
to leave the house and land. She was a big-hearted pleasant
girl and Thomas's uncle was very friendly with her. He was
always telling her that he had a fine handsome boy at home
himself and she'd never marry another man if she saw him.

'Musha,' she'd say, 'isn't it a pity he wouldn't come with
ye so I'd see him.'

'Have patience,' says Thomas's uncle, 'and if we stay
alive next year he'll be here with me."

'All right,' says she, 'don't forget it.'

As soon as the potatoes were dug each man put his spade
on his shoulder and then moved to the road. After the uncle
coming home, Thomas was there asking him questions about
the Tralee people. The uncle was glad telling him about
everything and above all about the young woman who was
so eager to see him.

'From where did she know me?' said Thomas, and he
wondering, and fancying to hear the story.

'Indeed, man, I was telling her about you and I think
she took great interest in my talk and,' said he, 'she told
me not to come again without you being along with me.'

'We have time enough to be thinking,' said Thomas.

'A look before us is better than two looks behind us,' said
the uncle, 'and may God put us right!'

The year coming to them, Thomas and the uncle were
very busy. He put a new suit in the making and fixed the
little house, because he had some thoughts in his head
nobody knew save himself and the uncle.

As soon as the start of the harvest came everyone was
readying himself, especially those who were going to face north

to Tralee. The morning they were going to go Thomas came
to his mother and told her that he was going to go with his
uncle north, and not to be worried or troubled if a while of
the year be spent before he would return. The poor mother
became sort of afraid, but she had no business interfering
with him; all she had to do was to let God's blessing on his
road. Then he said his farewell and took himself out the
door. He took with him his sickle and spade. The uncle
was ready before him and they went to the road. More and
more men were on the same road, each one shouldering his
own arms.

The coming Saturday they were standing as usual at the
Spalpeen's fair. They weren't long there when there were
farmers in plenty bargaining with them. But the uncle
didn't need to do much bargaining for he knew well the
man he was working for often before that, Thomas O'Brien.
As soon as the uncle saw him coming he welcomed him.

'I see,' said O'Brien, 'you have a stranger today with you.'

'I have,' said the uncle. 'We have use for more. Have
you a way for work for him?'

'I have and welcome,' said O'Brien. 'Come on.'

He had a horse and cart and he told them sit in and they
wouldn't be long going home. As soon as they were ready
he struck the horse and away with them. They weren't long
going to the house. As soon as they reached it the bright
welcomes were before them especially by the young woman
because of the stranger being with them. The young woman
was in a hundred pieces around them. Soon the dinner was
ready and herself sat to the table with them.

In the morning everyone was at his task for there was a
big field of wheat to be cut and they had to be working
hard. But that didn't leave them without companionship
and pastime. The young woman of the house, Margaret,
was there and among the boys that were there, there was

one very great with her. But since Thomas came to the house this boy was watching Margaret. He decided in his mind that she was making more friendly with Thomas than she was with him, and a sort of jealousy was coming on him.

Few nights but there would be company in O'Brien's house, especially since the outsiders came there. They were gathered there one night and they had dancing and singing going on. Thomas was a very nice singer and the young woman thought there was no better songster in the Province of Munster. She'd close her eyes and taste the sweetness of the words in the depth of her heart. She couldn't do that unbeknownst, however. Whoever noticed her, this boy I say didn't forget to put his eye on her. He got a fit in his heart, but he didn't say a word, but to bow down his head.

'By my palms, White John,' said a prattling old fellow who was trying to re-liven his pipe at the same time, 'but I'm afraid the man of the ash will put the man of the (turf) stack out.'

'O merry old pot-rack, 'tis for you this is,' said a sturdy fellow sitting near them.

'Musha, I leave it as a will to God, dear friend, that treachery is always in them, the women,' said White John. 'As we know, the poet didn't leave so much out when he said: "A woman who is made for one man and another woman who challenges all",' and he bowed his head down again and went thinking.

'Margaret, Margaret,' said he, and he hopped up standing and said in full voice to be heard the same by all who were present:

> 'If my love were through the centre of your heart
> As your love, and death, are destroying me,
> You'd walk mountains and heather glens for me
> To give a kiss or two from your heart to me,'

and in the batting of an eye he was clean beyond the door.

'The devil is done, and the Spotted Town is burnt!' said the man of the house, hopping up standing.

'Don't mind him, Dad,' said Margaret, 'there's nothing done.'

'O daughter of my soul,' said he, 'that good man is gone from the house in anger.'

'Don't mind that, Dad,' said she, 'there's a better man than him in this house tonight,' and she caught Thomas by the hand. 'Sing a song for me,' said she to him.

'The devil I won't have refusing you!' said Thomas and he started to sing 'Margaret Roche'.

He wasn't backward with it. He didn't sing a song so musically or truly in what was spent of his life. He didn't omit a syllable or a sound-beat. Everything was silent save the wind that was stirring the leaves of the old oak tree in the back garden. There was that much sweetness in his voice that he so moved old O'Brien that two tears ran down his cheeks.

When the harvest was saved and they had the potatoes dug it was time for the spalpeens to go to their own homes. There was nobody it was worrying more than Margaret. She didn't like to open the story to her father but her patience broke before Thomas and his uncle left the house.

'Dad,' said she, 'I am asking one request of you. I gave the love of my breast and soul entirely to that stranger that has been in the same house with us this while back. He is going in the morning with the rest of them, and what will I do after him? O! Dad, do something! Tell him not to go! I feel my heart slipping from me. I don't know at all if he goes what I will do.'

'Musha, O daughter of my soul, I am henceforth but an old tall-fellow, but I'd prefer you'd choose some other husband who'd have worldly property behind him. He's a good man without a doubt. I noticed him working amongst the men but if you'd do your own benefit you'd leave those thoughts aside. Oh! you'll get a better man than he and a budgetful of yellow gold!'

'Sun nor stars ever shone down on a better man, Dad, and every knuckle of his feet and hands is worth a budgetful of yellow gold.'

'It is ever said, O daughter, that a person prefers an inch of his will to a hand of his benefit. Have your will! He is a good man—I have no fault on him but that he is poor without property.'

'Musha, good is the father God gave me,' said she and she ran to him and spread her arms around him.

'You'd rather have Thomas now than me!' said he.

'Both of ye! Both of ye,' said she and the tears were coming from her eyes with joy.

Then the match was made and Thomas and Margaret O'Brien were married on the coming Tuesday. But alas, the mischief-maker was never silent. The coming year O'Brien met a man from Ventry parish and he was asking for Thomas. Envy of Thomas came in his heart, the luck he'd had, and he told O'Brien that he hadn't as a son-in-law but a contemptible widow's son who had no strength or vigour only his day's pay. When O'Brien heard this he thought the people in the west had no sauce with their potatoes³ only himself and that trifler of a spalpeen who stole the heart of his pet daughter he had on the hearth. Things would not be like that when he'd go home. He'd give them the ropes side of the house. He spoke to himself this way:

'Bad advice drives a person to the scaffold, but wasn't I big amongst the people west there until that trifler of a spalpeen came my way? But that soft foolish girl of a daughter I have was the cause of it, the guileless fool. I told

³ Meat or fish instead of potatoes only.

her that was how it would be, but she coaxed me with her babyish tears. But I'll have my revenge.'

When he came home he turned on the daughter. The poor girl gave him the best petting anyone ever got. She bought sweet cakes in the town for him but if she gave him honey on dishes she couldn't satisfy the angry devil inside him.

'Thomas,' said she one day, 'what my father has planned is to throw us out on the road. He has the spite in his nose for us this while back and choice doesn't go from the remedy. What I have planned to do is to fix the house in the corner of the farm if you would be satisfied and maybe, with the help of God, my father's anger would ebb yet.'

'All right, Margaret,' said he and they gathered their things and went to live in the small house. Poor Margaret was tormented but it was worse with her for Thomas.

'Have patience,' he'd say, 'for great is the value of patience. You'll have no want as long as God leaves me my health.'

They were passing life like that together, a while easy and a while hard, until the coming harvest. It was common at that time for people to be in contention with each other at all hours, trying to be the best man over each other. A man was no use without a party of hard men to back him up. A man whom a faction followed would be sooner received than great wealth with a man who had nobody behind him.

It happened that another farmer had a notice put up that he and his men would be in the town of Tralee on a certain day and that he expected O'Brien leading his men to be there. When O'Brien heard this he put together his men but didn't bother to call Thomas. On the morning of the fight he said to his wife, Margaret:

'This is a funny tale we have today. Your father is in danger of being killed without my being there to help him.'

'If there's treachery, it returns!' said she. 'My father was treacherous to you and how could you go in danger or jeopardy for him? Don't mind it.'

'Good against bad is the noblest action, little woman,' said Thomas. 'Come on with you! We'll go to the spot, whatever.'

Here's to the road with them when they were ready but when they came to the place of the fight they had nobody to see there but the fat strong hulk giving every twist to his blackthorn stick and every second shout from him that he was the one that routed O'Brien. Thomas strolled towards the Spalpeen's market. As luck in the world had it who should be there standing before him but his uncle and twenty-seven men of his near friends from Ballythomas with him and his own spade beside each man of them.

'O God of Powers, Thomas, where were you from the battle?' said the uncle. 'Such a beating and mixing I never saw! I was peering here and there but I didn't see you amongst the men. Where were you?'

'I was at home,' said Thomas. 'It seems he did not need my help.'

'Don't say that, Thomas,' said the uncle. 'Woe to the man in a country without one of his own for "On the fighting day the stick lays on his side." The stick was heavily laid on your wife's father today. He's over in there as gentle as a lamb. Don't you hear that man of the shouting down there ... the boasting he has about his heroism? Now is your time!' said he to Thomas. 'There's no man of these with me who will not go as far as gambling his soul for you. Go across over and tell him to come out.'

Thomas went over to where O'Brien was and caught him by the hand.

'Arise, man,' said he, 'we are not beaten yet. The man of the shouting won't take disgracing you beneath clay or stones with him!'

O'Brien was very unwilling because he had had more than enough of the day already, but Thomas was urging hard at him until he made him arise. They walked out then and Thomas let one loud shout out of him.

'Now is the time for the shouting people!' said he. 'O'Brien is here and where is the man who would nod his fist towards him? If that man be, now is his time!'

When the fat hulk of the shouting heard him he gathered to him his men and they came to where O'Brien was. O'Brien's men were not far from him, those who were not wounded, but they were only as a handful of straw compared with the twenty-seven men who were standing by Thomas's shoulder.

The big man gave a running charge at O'Brien, but he didn't succeed because Thomas put him eating the clay with a belt of a fist. There was never in the town of Tralee or since then any day of slaughter greater and the chasing and scattering of small birds was put on O'Brien's enemies.

When O'Brien himself saw that he had won and that Thomas was responsible, he had the shame of the world on him because of how much he had wronged him. He took him by the hand then.

'Forgive me!' said he. 'I did it black on you; but don't mind that now. Come home with me, and there's no danger that I'll antagonize you again as long as I live.'

He took with him Thomas and his spalpeens to his house, and believe me left them wanting nothing for a week. From that day Thomas and his wife, Margaret, were back in their own house again and often they all had company and pastime and conversation together.

CHAPTER FOUR

The Old Woman who Wronged her Son

It's a proverb 'That often a tailor promised and wouldn't come'. In my own youth there were country tailors in plenty, going from house to house, working. Often a tailor would have promised to you, and couldn't come for two months. There was none of them more talked about than John the Tailor. He was a man of fun and tricks, a man you wouldn't feel a long winter's night with, listening to him singing or telling long classical stories. It was said that there was no better story-teller in his time.

One night he was making a flannel vest for my father, there were a lot of people of the hamlet gathered into our house listening to him. I was small that time but I was old-wise enough to give a listening ear to the tailor. Up on the table he was sitting, with his legs crossed and his scissors, his measure, his thimble and his stick by him.

'Aye, tailor,' said the small smith, 'as it's you travels around most, it's your turn for a new story.'

'Indeed,' said the tailor, 'it's many a thing the like of me sees. As we know, the one who travels is storied and I'm one of that unlucky tribe, driven from place to place and from town to town, having a night here and a night there—at Oat Quarter last night, at Vicarstown tonight, and maybe in Glenfawn tomorrow night. But I tell you I saw one thing made me marvel, and made me cross too, and it often runs into my mind since.

'My grandfather was a good tailor. 'Twas he taught me my trade. I used to be with him in every house he worked in. It happened that we were working in a certain house.

Life wasn't too good then, and it was hard for poor people to live. The people of this house I say had very little income but whatever income there was the old woman of the house was often gaining out of it. Her daughter was married in the hamlet nearest to her. She had the full of the house of children and the mother used to be trying, naturally, to give her a little help known and unknown. Her son was married in the house and often the old woman and her son's wife used to be in each other's hair-combs. However,' said the tailor, 'myself and my grandfather were working hard. As soon as we had eaten the morning meal the young woman went from the house on some errand. When the old woman found the house to herself she started to hide a lot of things somewhere up in the room. There was no dozing on my grandfather because there was no move the old woman made but he was noticing; especially as he knew that many people suspected her to be causing the disturbance in the house.

'It was near on dinner-time when the young woman came home, and it was well on dinner-time for myself and my grandfather. But there was no purpose or attention being given to us. The hunger of the world was on me, and I was longing for the table to be set.

' "God with my soul, Grandad," said I, "is it how we came here to die of the famine?"

' "You are sharp in appetite, O son," said he, "but I'm afraid you'll have a long stand on weak legs."

'I was fit to faint when the young woman called home the people of the house. They were working in the field, and the field was a good piece from the house, and this woman was bone-lazy. All she did was to get up on the top of the fence and call on them at the top of her head and voice. When they came home my grandfather hopped down off the table and gathered to him his things.

' "Catch the head of that table!" said he, to the man of the house. They moved it over near a settle-bed in the corner. My grandfather sat on a chair at the head of the table and the man of the house sat beside him. Myself and the other man were sitting on the settle-bed. Indian-meal bread and milk was the meal we had. The bread was on the table but neither of the two women would bring the milk from the room, only every sharp word between them. My grandfather spoke:

' "Musha, morning agony on ye!" said he, "wouldn't one of ye bring the milk to us?"

' "'Tis not I will bring it to you, good man," said the young woman and she stood as straight as a guarding goat. "But let that thief in the corner take it with her as she takes everything. Let her have it, food and milk. 'Tis no use for my husband and me to try and live here when what's ours is raising another's family."

'There wasn't a gig out of the man of the house or his son. They were chewing at their best; but 'tis how there was shame and disgrace on them because myself and my grandfather were present. At last the old man's patience broke.

' "Little girl," said he, "you'd be better to have sense. There's nobody interfering with you or taking anything from you."

' "I say that you have it wrong," said the young woman. "'Tis unknown to you that life is passing, but it's not passing unknown to me, because 'tis me the shoe is hurting," and she stood up and went into the room where the old woman had the booty hidden. There wasn't a word from anyone but all our eyes were on the room. The old woman was sitting in the corner and a flame in her eyes like there would be in the eyes of a wildcat. It wasn't long until the young woman threw out a bag:

' "Look at that!" said she to the man of the house. "That is how your oaten meal is going! And look at this!" said she with another bag, "that is how your meal is going,' and she threw out a bag and another bag; "and honest man," said she to my grandfather, "is it any wonder for me to be talking?"

'Before the word was out of her mouth the old woman had jumped out of the corner, had a grip on the hair of her head and dragged her to the floor with her. Though the young woman was hard and strong, she couldn't get the upper hand of the old woman. We were looking at them raking each other, but nobody was inclined to go between them.

' "Your soul from the devil!" says my grandfather to the young man, "is there none of your wife's pain on you?"

' "Musha, I don't know what I should do, good man," said he. "They have me out of my mind."

' "It was said always," said my grandfather, "as near as his coat is to a man, nearer to him than that is his shirt. That's your way with you and your married wife."

'Then my grandfather sprang from his chair and grabbed the old woman and put her sitting in the corner.

' "Sit up there for yourself you little hag of mischief!" said he. "The people were right who said it was you were causing the disturbance. I'm watching you since morning unknown to you and I'm a witness to what you have done; and I admit that the young woman has all the right against you."

'He turned then to the old man of the house:

' "According to your conscience," said he, "let there be an end to this. You are the man of the house and it's you have to settle everything. It's a great shame for you to wrong your son and this poor girl who brought her purse of money to you. The poor couple have enough care without throwing what's theirs to others."

' "I admit you are completely right," said the old man, "and definitely, were it not for you, I wouldn't believe from the parish priest that they would have the like in them."

'From that day out and until the day they died, the angel of peace was among them.'

CHAPTER FIVE

A Man who was Clean in the Sight of People, but Unclean in the Sight of God

My love my Lord God! Isn't it straight and smooth life goes on according to His true holy will! Shouldn't we be joyful for His glorious light to be lit amongst us! Isn't there still many a person lying in the dark! God with us, Lord, isn't that a pity! I understand that there is no more valuable jewel in life than to have love for God of Glory, for I have gone through life and I see a lot that reminds me of the great power of God. I am here alone in this lonely place, looking back on the pleasant life I have spent and thinking on all the people who were there in my time and who are gone on the Way of Truth. May God grant them the eternal rest! It's hard news if the bush is in the gap before us. But the sinner's benefit is to be for ever in love with God, and not to be the same as a certain Peter.

This Peter was a mouthful among the parishes. He was important. There wasn't his better in his time. The man of the big heart, they called him. The tramp that went the road it was in Peter's house he stayed. He never let a person from his door without giving him lodging for the night. Its mark was on him; everyone was full of affection for him and on road and path there was only Peter on their lips.

But as we know, there's nothing but a while in this life for anybody, and Peter had only a while. On the day of his death it surprised the people when they saw the crowds coming to the house of his corpse. It happened that Michael Mannion was coming there. A tough, strong, courageous man was Michael, a man it would be difficult to put fear or fright on. When he was going the road east from the Hollow of the Sheep at the departing of day from night, he saw the rider meeting him on horseback. They saluted each other.

'Might I ask you, good man, where you are going?' said the rider.

'You might, certainly, stranger-man,' said Michael. 'Going to the wakehouse I am. The best man we had is stretched tonight and many a man and woman have moist eyes after him.'

'All of ye have great great woe after this man,' said the rider. 'Everyone I met on the way, they are sorry to be parting with him.'

'Oh! man of parts, there was none better than him. His going is the ruin of country and place and nobody was ungrateful to poor Peter, may God have mercy on his soul!' said Michael.

'Maybe somebody was, good man,' said the rider. 'But, whisper! would it be any hurry with you to go down in this glen down here and the big flagstone that's there, to lift it and look down under it? I promise you you'll see a thing that will amaze you. I will wait here until you come back.'

'By my own palms, it's no hurry, stranger-man,' said Michael, and jumped over the fence of the road.

When he went to where the flagstone was a sort of fear came on him, but he was loath to have any cowardliness come on him—a man as courageous as he. The flagstone was heavy but Michael succeeded in lifting it so that he saw clearly what was under it. It was barely that his soul didn't fall out of him when he saw it. 'Tis how a person's skeleton, unrecognizable, was lying under the centre of that flagstone!

He came to where the rider was, and amazement in him.

'Oh, good man,' said he, 'isn't it the queer place you sent me! When I lifted the flagstone 'tis how there was a person's skeleton lying under it, and it unrecognizable.'

'And do you know who put it there?' said the rider.

'I don't know from the land of the world who did the ugly deed,' said Michael.

'That man you and all praise! That's the man who did the bad act. He was clean in your sight but he was unclean in the sight of God. I tell you that praise from people is inconstant.'

He spurred his horse and left Michael there thinking to himself in the middle of the road.

CHAPTER SIX

A Woman who Forsook her Husband; a Fox and a Hen; and Other Matters

I remember well the fine summer's day my father took me south to the Flagstone Hollow. I was only a little girl at that time. The sun was shining beautifully and every place full of flowers. Out before us on the road there were sheep and the lambs dancing after them. The birds were merrily singing in the bushes that were growing on both sides of the road, and I running here and there, plucking blossoms and at the same time listening to the birds and looking at the young lambs dancing. It was well late when I reached Flagstone a little below Vicarstown, and those little things delayed me. It was a small thatched house there belonging to a person related to me named Patrick O'Kennedy. He was a small man but he had a roomy hospitable heart and he was good company. When night fell Eamonn and Thomas came in the door. They were next-door neighbours and one was no better than the other to make good company.

'Welcome, men,' said the woman of the house.

'May ye all live sound and alive!' said Eamonn in smart reply and he sat on a chair that was in the corner, threw a leg over one knee and started to put tobacco into his pipe.

'Have you any new tidings, Eamonn?' said Patrick, interrupting him.

'I haven't, musha, only Sean Dermot dying.'

'Musha, sound and alive be the teller!' said Patrick. 'The poor man! As we know, he wasn't too old yet.'

'He wasn't,' said Eamonn, 'and it's now he'd be better off because of the inheritance that came to him from America.'

'Indeed,' said Thomas, 'isn't it fine Brigid Connor heard that it came to him!'

'She heard,' said Patrick. 'What is not heard?'

'Musha, she not leaving him be!' said Eamonn. 'As if it wasn't time for her to come to him! She didn't stay with him when he was young and strong.'

'Oh, a good hurler is the man on the fence,' said Thomas. 'As we know, nobody ever had enough sense, especially young people. They want nothing but their own way. Sean was a quiet, sensible boy, too, with only one fault on him, that is, being poor without land or riches and Brigid was young and airy when she married him. There was nothing making her dizzy only being married to Sean, like a lot of other girls.'

'And did she know, Thomas,' said Mary, the woman of the house, 'that Sean Dermot had no means when she married him?'

'Yah, the poor girl didn't know anything about it,' said Patrick. ''Tis how a wrong was done on her. There was a woman related to Sean married to a man from Milltown. He was a pedlar. They had a donkey and cart and they used to be going from place to place selling pins and needles and a lot of other goods. When they'd have the full of the cart sold, they'd go to the town of Tralee because that was the best place they'd get the little articles they wanted. It happened that the woman related to Sean got to know Brigid Connor who was a servant girl in the house they stayed in. She would be coaxing and advising her to give up service and saying there was a fine good-looking boy related to herself in Ventry parish and if she'd care to marry him she'd have a life more happy and satisfied.

'The poor girl was heeding her, no wonder, because she often would tell her that service was the worst; there was nothing worse than being under the hand of other people. A little while after that the friendship started between them because Sean got a letter that was full of love. Though he never saw Brigid something in that letter awoke in his heart something he never felt before that. "By gor", he said to himself, "I'll pay her a visit and I'll know what sort of a woman she is." Then he went to his relative woman and asked her about the young woman—where she was living and a lot of other questions. When he had some information, he dressed himself up and faced the road to Tralee. Nobody knew where Sean was gone until he came home and Brigid Connor married with him.

'There wasn't as much talking done about any couple married in eight years before as was done about Sean Dermot and Brigid Connor. At market and fair there wasn't in the people's mouth but the pair.

'It's for ever said that the three things that run swiftest are a stream of water, a stream of fire, and a stream of falsehood, and a lot of falsehood was being mixed through the whisper-lisper that was going on. Brigid was very young and it was easy to disguise a calf on her, especially as she was a stranger, not mixing with people.

'It was in Sean's house the young girls of the hamlet used to be gathered since Brigid came there. Often they'd have conversation and company afoot and it would go very hard with Brigid when she'd see Sean so great with them. She'd often be watching him under the eyelashes unknown to him and she'd say to herself, "Sean is making more friendly with other young women than with me!" and a kind of jealousy was coming on her. Sean hadn't a notion that anything like that was worrying her. It's difficult to put a wise head on a young body, and another thing, Brigid was a girl from a town and wasn't used to country ways or the country work that goes with it, and it wasn't long until the poor girl tired of it. On Saturday morning she spoke to Sean:

' "I'm going home for a while, Sean," she said, "and I hope you'll not be great with any other woman until I return."

' "All right," said Sean, "it will do you good to pay a visit to your people. A person is like that at first after marriage and especially in a strange place. But I'll be lonely until you come again."

'But Sean had a long loneliness on him because Brigid didn't return after a week, or after a fortnight, or after a year, nor for forty years after that.'

'Musha, wasn't it of him she made the fool!' said Thomas.

'She made a greater fool than that of him,' said Patrick, 'because she wrote a letter to him five years after she left him which told him to come for her and she'd come home with him. The poor deluded man went east to the town of Tralee. She was there before him, without a doubt, and she was nice and kind to the poor fellow, as though true. Sean thought the rising sun on a fine autumn morning no brighter than she when he saw her coming towards him in the street. My poor man spread out his arms and thanked God who brought him his way. He put the bright welcomes before her. All the youngsters of the street were looking at the poor simpleton, making fun of him, but poor Sean thought, no wonder, that it was some sport they had going on. He wasn't used to the likes of them, and therefore he had no great interest in them.

'When they had done a lot of talking and discussed life as they wished, she took him with her and she never stopped until she came to the most backward and miserable place in the town of Tralee, and she left him there, a foolish article, not knowing which way to go, east or west. At last he found someone who guided him.

'When he came home he wouldn't tell his tale to anyone, but the thing he'd say was: "To the devil I give my share of the women, anyway!" '

'He had his piece said,' said Thomas, 'but 'tis not on him alone that ailment is. It's too easy for him to find a partner.'

'The poor man was falling and rising with life, like many,' said Patrick. 'He had a nice prosperous house and a small garden. He was living happily but when the inheritance came to him he wasn't in the same place since. I suppose the poor man's heart rose up in him. Seven hundred pounds was a big lob of money, coming unexpectedly. It was riches and as we know it gave many something to talk about because it was the hope unthought of. The story went from mouth to mouth until Brigid heard it, who was then an old woman. What do you say to her,' said Patrick, 'but that she didn't decide to come to Sean? On a summer's day Sean was up on top of the hill footing turf. It wasn't of Brigid Connor he was thinking but of his money pennies. He was for ever thinking how best to deal with it. He spent the day like that, working and thinking. It was the hunger that first made him move from his worryings.

' "God with my soul!" said he, "I have the day spent! The sun is sliding down over the hills."

'He caught the old jacket that was thrown on the bank and didn't stop until he reached the house. The arrangement of servant or horse wasn't on the hearth before him and he himself had to fix the fire. He was sitting on the chair with his back down to the door when he found somebody coming in. He turned around and saw a nice middle-aged woman standing near the table. He stood up to give her charity, for he thought she was a travelling-woman. When he came to her with a small plate of potatoes, she looked at him and sniggered—"Sean, my pet, it's no charity I want."

'Arrah, friend of my soul, he was startled, because the sound of her speech reminded him of something.

' "And what do you want?" said he.

' "Is it how you don't recognize me?" said she.

' "I don't recognize you, woman," said Sean, in wonder, "How do I know who you are—and I don't care—but be going."

' "It's not for that I came," said she.

' "And what else, if so?" said Sean.

' "To look after you, my pet, for the rest of our lives! Am I not Brigid, your wife, and 'tis how I came to stay with you."

'A burst of anger swelled in Sean's heart and he told her, in words he was never taught in school, to be out of the house. She dug her foot down that she wouldn't go out for him, but he took her by the shoulder, and threw her out the door.

' "May you never leave me alone!" said he, "if it's not time for you to come to me at the end of my life! And 'tis not to me you were coming but to my money! But 'tis little of it you'll have, whoever will. I'd rather throw it in the river's stream than possess you of any of it, you little hag!" and he closed the door on her.

'She had to clear off, and he didn't see her since.

'Awhile after that a brother's daughter came to look after him. The poor man is failing and someone will have a good hoard after him.'

'There's nobody has more right to it than the young girl who is minding him at the end of his life,' said Mary.

'That's true,' said Patrick. ''Tis said "My love you when you have something." Small fear but it will be well watched.'

The next morning there was no drowsiness on Patrick. He was up early to change the cattle from the night-field.

A little after him his wife, Mary, arose and was busy seeing to the duties of the morning. She was making so much noise and racket that I woke up. All the noise surprised me.

'What's wrong with you, Mary,' said I, 'that you're making all the noise?''

'The devil of a fox, musha, my pet,' said she. 'There isn't a hen or a duck in the place but he has carried away after the night.'

'You don't care if he didn't sneak up on your own little hens!'

'Musha, long straying on him!' said she. 'He has my big spotted hen after the night, a hen I wouldn't allow for half a sovereign, and I suppose he has more,' and she went from me with some food on a dish. You'd hear her half a mile from home calling the hens. But her object was to get the big hen.

I was up and at the fireside when she came in.

'Did you find her?' said I.

'I didn't, my pet, nor I won't,' said she. 'The twister is too cute for me. He takes a bite with him on his visits always. They're gone from Kate down here, too.'

'It's a great thing that he didn't make ye envy each other!' said I.

'Arrah, girl, if he took three of them it wouldn't pain me any—but my fine hen—and I after giving my gold crown for herself and a dozen eggs over there at the harbour last year!'

'May naught but she go from you,' said I.

'Oh! yes indeed, my pet, it's fine and easy you have it! I hate the scolding I'll get from Patrick more than anything. He doesn't have anything to say to me only that I don't secure the little shed any way properly on them. But I thought if he was the accursed one himself, that he couldn't reach them last night.'

'Oh! Mammy, Daddy is coming, and the tea not ready for him!' said little Thomas, the small son who was standing in the doorway.

'God welcome him, my pet,' said she, 'God welcome him!' and with that Patrick came in, after bringing the cows home for milking. Mary was busy preparing the tea.

'Bring the cups over with you,' said she to me.

I hopped over the floor fussing and put the appearance of work on me. Patrick was sitting on a chair at the head of the table without a gig from him. It was seldom with him to be so quiet, because he was a nice, chatty, pleasant little man. Mary moved over to him.

'In the account of God, Pat,' said she, 'the fox took two hens from me last night. But what is the importance to me only the big spotted hen that I was saving! I wouldn't allow, for Ireland, that she'd be taken!'

'Don't be bothering me with your hens!' said Patrick, and anger in his voice.

'What's this crankiness on you?' said Mary, and she stood before him like a soldier.

'It is that you should be ashamed to treat so a ridge of new potatoes, knowing well you could get no potato there yet. But if you wanted them why didn't you dig them properly and not give them a pig's rooting?'

Mary stopped and looked him between the two eyes. 'Musha, are you serious?' said she. 'Doesn't your heart know that I had nothing to do with them?'

'Go west and look at them,' said he, 'and you'll see the trace of your work.'

That speech took the memory of the hens from her mind, and she didn't wait to eat enough food, but to go out and go to where the spoiling was done. That was for her to be seen, without doubt. There were a lot of stalks broken and the place around them torn and little hollows here and there in the ridge. She started to gather the clay in to the bottoms of the stalks, because the new potatoes weren't ripe yet. In the covering she came across some hard lump under the clay. She scooped the clay out of the way and what was it but the big hen, hidden by the fox for himself for the coming night. Here she came, in, at the end of her soul, with the hen in her hand.

'Look, cross one,' said she, 'what did the spoiling! The devil of a fox did it, and mischance to him! if he killed her, he didn't succeed in eating her!'

A kind of shame came on Patrick over the scolding he had given his wife.

'Musha, a cause to laugh for us, wife,' said he, 'as Peter said long ago when he found the ass drowned!'

I plucked the hen myself and we put it boiling. Myself and Patrick ate every scrap of it for Mary couldn't taste of it because it was the fox that killed it.

We spent that day happy and content together, but when the night came, whatever spurred Patrick, he put the horse into the Slab Field, tethered. The poor man didn't understand that it was dangerous for him there, but it's afterwards all acts are understood. The small field was very dangerous altogether, because there was a deep hollow in one end of it and no shielding fence between the horse and the hollow, and whatever reaching over he did at the edge of the hollow he fell and broke his back, may they be safe where it's told!

When Patrick went for him the next morning to bring him home, it was on his poor heart the hard grip came, for he had nothing else in life but his children and his horse. He was cold poor then, the poor man, unable to put his hand in his pocket to alter matters.

When he came to the house with the bad news Mary nearly lost her mind. Poor people who are not succeeding in life are a great pity. They are vexed and maltreated.

Patrick and Mary were in dire straits for years after that, contending with a bare hearth and a pack of young children, with only two little donkeys to work. Often Mary was on the road and the two donkeys in front of her, turning to do work with them. But it's true that dearest to God is a poor vexed person. They were striving along until the eldest son grew up in age and ability. He went into service with a farmer in the neighbourhood, and in two years he had managed to have enough money earned to buy a young horse for his father, coupled with whatever scraping he himself was able to do.

It's on poor Mary the joy was when the young horse came to the house, because she made out that she had seen the last of life's hardship. Her family was grown; one was in service and two more able to help their father and that lightened the yoke and the heartbreak for herself.

They were spending life in comfort together, but when a person thinks it's nice 'tis how it's a mocking trick. It was that same way with Mary for when she had life at its best her head was brought low. A bout of sickness struck her husband, Patrick, and he spent a year on his bed, and not improving. He died unexpected by Mary. That left her hardship for the rest of her life. It's often I used to pay her a visit because I was closely related to her. Though life was hard for her, she didn't lose the fine, wide laugh or the big, generous heart.

CHAPTER SEVEN

The Snail-Trick; Tommy Griffin's Death; a Wake

In the neighbourhood near us there was a little small man whose name was Tommy Griffin. He was a stocky, strong fellow and had the name of being an able man. He had a nice little farm of land and the luck of this life was good with him. But he had the worst fault any man or woman ever had—he hadn't the heart of a mouse. He never once gave a dish of potatoes to a tramp of the roads, or a cup of milk. We used to be often in his house, spending the evening, when we were young girls, growing up. He had the wife who was the best that ever broke bread, and that's a big word, but Tommy had a rod on to her. I often saw her sneaking a dish of potatoes to old Kit, a travelling woman who used to be coming to the hamlet that time. Poor old Kit was a great woman for fun and we used to have the fun of the world on her. She had a lot of tricks and it's by her I saw the snail-trick being done for the first time ever. She made Kateen Michael get a basin full of dry sand. Two more went out full of excitement, looking for the snail— it was easy to get one that time. They came in and they had a big, black snail.

"'Tis you are youngest and will marry soonest,' said she to Maura Shaun. 'Put the snail in the basin and at the end of half-an-hour we'll know the name of the boy who will have you as a wife.' We all started to laugh.

'Arragh, wise woman, where will the poor snail get pen

and ink to write with?' said Maura, and a big red face on her with shame.

'Oh indeed it's no laughing,' said old Kit, and she put the snail down on the basin. She got a red handkerchief then and she spread it as a sheet across the basin. She spoke a couple of words under her breath, low, but we didn't understand her at all. She left it for a nice while then without moving it.

'Yes, little girls, move close to me!' said she, and she lifted the sheet.

We were all around the table then without a word from anyone but peeping over each other's shoulders into the basin.

'Your soul from the spots I know who he is!' said little Breeda when she saw the little roads the snail had made on the top of the sand, as if the letters 'P' and 'M' were written on the sand by him.

The laughing started again. We all tried that funny trick; but it wasn't for need of its magic we were; youth was in power with us that time.

Old Kit was full of tricks and of course we wouldn't prefer a piper coming the way to her. But Tommy never gave hospitality to her nor to anyone else, just as little.

It's well I remember the day he was dying in a high bed in the corner. It was a little straw-roofed house he had and the little house was full of people who were after coming to inquire for him. He took a start out of them when he spoke:

'My friends and relatives, I am clearing off,' said he, 'and let neither regret nor sorrow be on any one after me, because, by certainty, I didn't earn it. I got from God every best jewel any poor person ever got, wealth and health, but sharp alas! I did not use them correctly. But Oh my Lord! you played me foul! You gave me everything, but you didn't give me the heart!' and he put a shout from him you would hear at the other side of the hamlet.

The neighbours all ran in but he was dead before them.

Myself and Kate Jim thought it long until night would come and we would be waking him. When we went in the corpse was stretched in the bed and eleven candles lighting at its foot and there was another candle that wasn't lighting.

'I wonder is he a danger to us?' said Kate. 'Isn't it the ugly appearance he has!'

'Oh, didn't you ever hear that death puts his own appearance on everybody?' said I.

'I'm afraid of him!' said Kate. 'I won't go near him. I'll say my prayer here.'

The soldiering was in me.

'I'll go over and I'll strike my hand on his cheek,' said I, because I heard my mam saying it, that if you struck your hand on a dead person you wouldn't have any loneliness on you.

'But, Peig, why is the other candle not lit?'

'I know it well,' said I. 'That's the candle that's standing up in place of Judas, the one who betrayed our Saviour. The other eleven are standing for the rest of the apostles. They are guarding the corpse from the enemy who is outside.'

'Oh, the Cross of God between us and him, Peig, may God not allow that he'll have anything to do with poor Tommy!'

'God allows a lot of things, Kate,' said I, 'but avoid evil and you have no danger. But, Mary! Isn't the human queer! Isn't it nice and chatty Tommy was four nights ago! And see now the way he is! I'll bet, Kate, the person who stole the shirt off the bush from your mother a few days ago, it didn't strike into his mind that he'll be like Tommy!'

'Oh, it's true for you, Peig, but nobody has enough sense. See the old women, what they're up to! What will they be doing?'

'I suppose, Kate, it's keening they'll be,' said I.

'Oh, Peig, I'd rather that I stayed at home!'

'Don't mind that,' said I, 'it's the fate of everybody. Don't you see the old women—isn't it little Kate Michaeleen thinks of it? See the way she raises his head on the pillow. There's nothing affecting us only youth. A day will come on us yet, if we live for it, when we won't be afraid.'

'I don't know in the world, Peig, but I'm afraid enough now, whatever happens. I don't like seeing the face of the dead. I don't know what was on me and to come at all! Wouldn't I have the company over at home playing *puirins*[1] or imitating old Kit. You'd better go with me, Peig, and we'll both go over and we'll stay together until morning!'

'Don't mind that, but do what I say. Of course, it's not right for anyone to go by a wake-house, or to go from it without having somebody with him. We'll stay another while. Tea will be going on immediately. The old women are fixing themselves up for it.'

'The old women are great people for tea, Peig.'

'That's true for you, Kateen, but I'd say they've a greater love for tobacco. It's only a couple of nights ago since my father was saying it, that himself saw a woman in Ventry parish who sold her shawl for a half-quarter of tobacco.'

'Musha, wasn't she the fool, Peig? I've a great love for tea but that's a thing I wouldn't do.'

'On my soul, Kate, there are odd women in this parish who'd do it.'

'Musha, it's hard to guess between them. They have a great liking for both of them.'

As we were talking who would come down across but Big Nell, the woman of the house.

'Musha, the joy of my heart for ever, both of you, children,' said she. 'Move up to the fire. You're perished with the

[1] A form of Blind Man's Buff.

cold, but you'll have a cup of tea immediately and a hunk of white bread. Little girls have the liking of the world for white bread and jam.'

We moved up to the corner and I felt that Kate was very unwilling. But when we were seated in the corner a little while, we were very comfortable in it.

'Let's not go home at all, Kate!' said I, 'we'll have company here. We'll be listening to the old people telling stories and the old women will be telling each other about their affairs.'

'I don't know, musha, Peig. I'd rather be asleep.'

'Don't say that, Kate. Didn't you hear what Tommy said the night he was telling us the story—that we should guard him well when he'd be laid out. But that night he didn't expect death this soon.'

'O he didn't, the poor man! But death is a coward who often comes without being expected,' said Kate.

'Yes, Kate, it was true for the poet when he said this verse:

> My eye closed and weak is my sense.
> There is weakness in my limb, a white stocking under
>   my jaw.
> Women will not long have wailing after me
> And long will the corpse of faults be feeling torment.,

'O God be with us, stop and don't make me lonely.'

'Here, down with you,' said Nell, 'and enjoy this grand red jam.'

'Musha, it's said ever,' said I to myself, 'what a person doesn't spend himself, his enemy spends it.'

We went down helter skelter, and we had an edge on our teeth, because it was a long time before that since we saw the like.

When everything was put to one side Big Nell said it would be a good thing to say the Rosary for Tommy's soul and the souls of the dead. Before the Rosary was finished Kate was asleep soundly with her little mouth open. If I were to be hanged I couldn't keep from laughing. When Big Nell heard me laughing in my prayer she threw a sod of turf on me, but it wasn't to do me any harm she did it, the poor woman. When Kate awoke it was bright day and we both went home together.

It is true the mouth of the grave gives to the needy one, and it was the same way with Big Nell. Tommy had a rod on to her but well the creature suffered it. No one heard her complaining. The man of greatest wealth who ever lived had nothing to get in the end but 'the scarce six feet in some graveyard'. Tommy was buried and all he had in the world stayed with Big Nell and it was she had sport from it. She used often say 'What is gathered meanly, it goes badly.' Big Nell never let anyone go from her door hungry and God gave her all her heart would wish for as long as she lived.

CHAPTER EIGHT

A Boat-Load of Turf brought from Iveragh during a Gale of Wind

The weather is beautiful and the sun is shining brightly on sea and on land. There is freshness and brightness in everything God created. The sea is polished, and the boys are swimming down at the shore. The little fishes themselves are splashing on the top of the water and even the old people are sitting out here and there sunning themselves. Poor humans are overcome after the winter because we have a hard life of it on the island for that part of the year—hemmed in like a flock of sheep in a pen, buffeted by storm and gale, without shade or shelter but like a big ship in the middle of a great sea, cut off from the land without news coming to us or going from us. But God does the ordering, praise for ever to Him, when He sees our hardship. He abates the storm, and gives us the opportunity to go among the people, and when the summer and fine weather like this come He takes from us the memory and the gloom of winter.

See myself here, sitting on the fence, looking around me and thinking on the hundreds of things that are gone. I see the change that has come in life in my own memory, the importance and the snobbery. There are white stockings on burned heels today and the back of the hand given to the customs and manners of the old and an alternative life being led. It can't be helped, I suppose, because life is changing as the years are passing along.

When I look to the south on Dingle Bay, that place

reminds me of the time I was a little girl by the fire, listening
to the old people reminiscing and describing to each other
the troubles and the hardships they had gone through. I
used to hear my father, may God have mercy on his soul!
saying frequently that the worst of trades is the fishing
because there is no hardship in the world worse than the
hardship that follows it. He was a fisherman himself, and
the old people who used to spend the evening with him were
fishermen. I'm looking at them again, I think, and listening
to them raising the sweet, tasty Gaelic. My father is again
alive before me, describing the hardship. I see the sensible
head being nodded, emphasizing his story to Maurice.
Though he wasn't tall he was broad and strong and
intelligent, and he was great at telling a story.

'Yes, Maurice,' said he, on a certain night, when they
were sitting by the fire. 'The proverb is true: "Don't spread
your cloak any further than you can cover it." '

'To what do you say that, Thomas?' said Maurice.

'Because I saw a lot who spread their cloak far and fast,
and they finished miserably afterwards. When I was living
in Kilmacdowney, before I came here, I had a small bit
of land. As you know, the Lady, Betty Rice, was the mistress
over us and to tell the truth, she was good in a way, but
she was the very devil in other ways. Her control was as
fast and as firm over those who were under her hand as
the control of Queen Maeve of Connaught long ago. Anything she decided to do, there was no business going against
her, especially for those under her control. If they went
against her they were finished with land and tenancy. In
the heel of the hunt the Lady decided to buy a big boat
and bring it with her from Galway and she picked eight of
the best men under her hand as a crew for the boat.
McEligott was the Captain, and a clever man who was well
used to the sea. She presented the boat to them only to

obey her every time she would need the boat. I was a
member of the team myself; she decided on me because
I was hard and strong at that time. But alas! it's often I
didn't boast about it because many a narrow escape I went
through while I was following it. My blood shakes when I
think of the hardship I went through.'

'Ah, there's trouble and hardship following the fishermen always,' said Maurice.

'There is,' said my father, 'and they lose by it often, God
help us. I remember well a year we were without any turf,
because of the summer being bad. There was the draught
of the world through the big house, and there must be firing
in plenty there. One day the Lady decided to send us for a
boat-load of turf to Iveragh. Though we had the unwilling-
ness of the world, there was no business giving her a refusal.
When we found the morning calm, and, as we thought,
without any danger for crossing the Bay to Iveragh—'

'Not coming before you in your speech,' said Maurice,
'I suppose there's a good distance between Cahir Quay
and Goleen?'

'On my oath, there is, my boy, but we had a good boat
and the sea calm. But as the proverb said "It's not the same
to go to the King's house as to come from it". That's the
way it was with us, because going in the mouth of Goleen,
the wind turned and it wasn't long till storm and sea was
exhausting us. But we were hard and strong and we rowed
her with the dint of strength, besides the help of God.

'We reached the harbour beyond, but we'd no great
jubilation in us because we were exhausted from rowing;
but since we had dry land now we thought nothing of it.
There were welcoming, friendly people before us and they
didn't let us lay the tip of a finger on the boat—they put
her on a safe side themselves.'

'There are good people in Iveragh always, it seems.'

'It's there the best of men are,' said my father, 'not to mention the women. I couldn't criticize them anyway. When the boat was out of danger they were tearing us apart, trying to bring us to their own houses. But it was no use for them because Maurice O'Shea wouldn't let us go with anyone. He took us with him to his own house, and he didn't leave thirst or hunger or cold on us. Maurice had a generous welcoming house and it was hard for a wanderer to get by it. Although he had only a small bit of land and a nice comfortable thatched house he was living as satisfied as if he had wether and ducks; and of course he had a housewife if ever any poor man had. She had a vast generous heart and they had no want in life but one thing, that is, they had no one in family, but the Angel of Peace was between them, and that was a big thing.

'We spent that night happily, but neither the following day nor the day after that was calm to go across and we were getting impatient. Another thing about it, we were ashamed to be pushing in on Maurice because he wouldn't let any man of us away from him. It's what he used to say: "Don't have any question on you, men! There's enough for twelve in my house, with no grudge. You'll want for nothing until you're able to go home."

'On the morning of the second day, the weather was neither calm nor kind, but when we had eaten the morning meal, Lena, the woman of the house, said to her husband, Maurice:

' "I'm going to Cahir today to visit my sister because she has a young baby, but don't you forget these men. Let them have no thirst nor hunger," said she.

' "Musha, you are a good housewife, may God reward you for your work," said McEligott.

' "Good man," said she, "God gave us all we have and ordered us to help the wanderer."

'When she was ready to go, she turned on her heel.

' "I hope you'll be happy together until I return," said she, and off she went.

'But if she went, there was a good man in charge of the house, and he wasn't the wisp in the place of the brush. When he milked the cows he'd throw the milk in the cream-crock. There was a little hole in the crock with a bung stuck in it and it was often during the day that Lena was away from the house that Maurice drew the bung to give milk to the men, in case they'd be thirsty, and as he put the milk above in, so he'd draw it out below.

'When Lena came home, and when she had the cows milked, she went to the crock with the milk but there wasn't a quart in the bottom of it. When she came in she was chuckling.

' "Not a drop of milk did you put in the crock since, Maurice," said she.

'He looked at her, and said: "By the pipe of the white gander, Lena, the author of good deeds wouldn't put it up over the bung. As I'd put it in above, so I'd take it out below."

' "You're a good man, and I like you now more than ever," said Lena, "God is good from today till tomorrow, and these men will be going home tomorrow with God's help."

'It was true for her. The morrow was beautiful and the sea was calm and the boat wasn't long being filled with turf. When we were ready we gave our hearty thanks to Maurice O'Shea and Lena, his wife. Then we set two sails on her and we had a nice following wind until we moved a good bit over from the mouth of Goleen. Then we noticed that the Bay wasn't as kind as we thought it was because a blast of wind came that made the sails rattle.

' "I'm afraid, men, that we won't have over or hither now," said McEligott. "The boat is too deep and the sea is not too quiet. The wind is strengthening and the way is too long."

' "And what have we to do?" said Sean Foley.

' "As best we can, my boy," said McEligott "The help of God and our own help. We haven't the second way out of it but to put the turf into the sea. If we don't do that there is no way the boat could run the sea and it swelling and rising already."

'Well, as we worked on the turf, throwing it overboard, the boat was taking water and were it not for how hard we worked and how soon we had the boat empty, I don't think we would have reached land at all.

'There wasn't a man or a woman, old or young, who wasn't out to Barque Point. Even the lady herself, Betty Rice, she was the person furthest out. She was sorry because it was herself had put us in danger. They could barely see the boat at all, because the sea was in white waves. But I suppose we were not to be drowned,' said my father. 'The Glorious King was in favour to us, because coming in for Barque Point a huge wave threw itself in on us without pity or mercy and swept with it Sean Foley. I myself saw him going west with his mouth wide open blowing brine in the sky and trying to catch a hold on the boat. I jumped up, because I didn't mind my death or my life from that moment. I stretched out as far as I could; I never strained myself as much. There wasn't in the boat of me only my two feet. By the grace of God I caught hold of the top of his head just when he was being swept down to the bottom. Two more of the crew came to my aid and we hauled him into the boat. The poor fellow was a bald-drowned mouse, but he didn't mind since he was free again amongst the men.'

' "Your pulse is my music, Thomas!" said McEligott. "That's a good deed you've done. I am sure we're from danger now, with God's help, because the Point is only three boat lengths from us. Wasn't it a bad wave! It didn't leave a stick in the hand of any man of us."

' "It didn't, or sense in anyone's head either," said Martin Big Ted.

' "Don't say that, Martin," said McEligott. "Wasn't the sense good that stayed with Thomas Sayers?"

' "I don't care what sense stayed with Thomas. There didn't stay a spark of it in my head. I thought I was being swallowed to the floor of the sea."

' "Aroo! and weren't we too, you silly?" said Pat Dermot.

' "Musha, God bless my soul, Lord," said Sean Foley, "wouldn't I get the ugly death being eaten by the worms of the sea!"

' "I will to God that it was nearly not only you they'd have," said Martin. "But you are your own grief and nobody else, Sean."

' "Ye may talk now," said McEligott, "but there wasn't a murmur out of any of you when you had the knock over the brain a moment ago."

'In the midst of the turmoil what was I thinking on only the sermon the priest had, the Sunday before that, and he giving out about what happened to the boat on the Lake of Galilee long ago. That gave me courage because I knew that the same Law was looking down on ourselves and that we wouldn't be in danger.

'When we reached Barque Point, exhausted and wet, Betty Rice was the first person to catch hold of the stern of the boat.'

'I suppose she was frightened, and no wonder,' said Maurice, fixing himself on the chair.

'She was, and especially because it was for herself we were working, but sharp alas! it is we were not grateful to her. As soon as I put the soles of my two feet on the dry land I swore black oaths that I wouldn't go into that boat as long as I lived again. She wasn't hard on me about it, because of the accident that happened to us, but it is said that the King never lost a man yet but he could get another in his place. On the morrow there was another man in my place and it's on me there was no sorrow about it. I thought at first that it wouldn't be so easy for me to give the refusal to the mistress, but when I explained the story from start to finish, she admitted that I was right and she left with me my little patch of land. Everybody thought I'd be thrown out on the side of the road but it's not as is thought that things be. It is how she took great pity on me.'

'It is said and it is true,' said Maurice, 'that after the oaths the women are best.'

'That's true, Maurice,' said my father, and he poked the fire. 'She didn't flourish for long after that. A bout of sickness came on her and didn't part with her for two years until she died. I don't know from life how her worldly wealth went, but all of its signs today is the big flagstone that is over her grave in Ventry graveyard.'

'The clock in the churchyard lives, but the hand that placed it there doesn't.'

'Yes,' said my father, 'and woe to him who accepts defeat in case it may be difficult for him to return.'

Maurice got up and knocked the ash from his pipe.

'You'd never tell me that it might be time for me to go home,' said he.

'Indeed, Maurice, I only want your company. Don't you know we'll be long enough asleep. We'll soon have sleep without awakening, though we do our best.'

That much was true for him. They're asleep now, may God grant them everlasting life, and to every dead soul! I am an old woman watching to go asleep in the same place, no one knows when, but may God smooth the long road for us all!

CHAPTER NINE

The Story of Betty Kelly's Son and his Bright Love

On sitting here by the door three little boys ran west by me. There's another boy after them trying to catch up with them. They remind me of the time myself and Kate Jim were running down the road long ago. It was merry we were with the summer sun shining down on us. Down the road with us, Kate before me and I at an easy trot after her.

The crossroad was full of people. Betty Kelly's son was there, after coming home from South America and the people of the parish were before him at the crossroad. Betty had only him, and as we know she held him in big esteem. The proverb didn't leave so much out—that 'Its own child is bright to the carrion crow.'

The son wasn't long home when it happened to him that he fell in love with a fine handsome girl named Nance McDonagh. Isn't it queer that love makes a person blind? Because the same thing happened to Nance. The poor girl had no spark of sense after him and it was said by everyone that they'd make a fine couple.

The game was on a long time before it reached Betty's ears, and the parish wasn't any the better for it when she heard it. She mixed Hell and God's Heavens. She spoke bad, hard, and bold to Nance McDonagh and told her that she was no equal for this Tim of hers, and she laid it down flat for her to finish with him. Poor Nance was in a fix and that talk lay greatly on her mind. It was worse it lay on Tim, for next morning he wasn't on his bed or in the parish. The people of the hamlet thought he had gone off his head and away with them looking for him. They didn't leave a cliff or cave from Ridge Head to Sheep Hollow unsearched for him, but his trace was not to be had. Betty was a great pity. She had no spark of sense, up on the fence and calling aloud on Tim to come home and she'd never say a bitter word again to him about Nance.

But Tim was the length of her call from her. The police and the people of the parish were looking hard for him, but they failed.

What goes long goes cold. Tim's memory was leaving the people's mind, but not so with poor Nance. His memory was as much alive in her head as ever it was. She would be in with Betty, and telling her that she couldn't let it into her mind that Tim had died.

'What makes you so sure of that?' Betty would say with the tears in her eyes.

'God, praise for ever to him, wouldn't allow such a bad end to Tim! He wouldn't, I say! He is still alive somewhere in the world.'

'If he was alive, Nance, he'd write—but he's not! The years are slipping by without news from him. Isn't that two years gone already?' and a burst of grief came on her. Only for Nance McDonagh she would go out on the fence and sing her old lonesome dirge. Wasn't it often in the last year she was up on that fence with these words going:

'My feet are burnt
In blisters scalded
From walking these long roads of the King,
Seeking my treasure
Of a musical boy
Who had the bloom of the rose on his cheek.

Oh! love and bright pet
How sad the story
And I don't know where you go!
You'll hear no call from me
Or sound of my shout
And you take no notice of my weeping eye!

O loving boy
Quiet, fresh, and gentle,
Your laugh was nice, as was your glance,
Who promised your mother
To stay by her
But it was the head of curls put you astray.

And where is the damsel
In forest or seclusion
Could keep a nice quiet boy like you
Who would leave her
As you left me
Who would not be lamenting and shedding tears?'

But Nance made her sit on the stool in the corner.

'Nance,' said she one day, 'may God reward the graces
on you! Only for you it's long ago I would be where the
herring lives in his nest. If I understood the position that
time as I do now, Tim wouldn't be away, and your heart
broken as it is—and I'm the cause of it! But it's true that
it's after every act it's understood.'

'Have sense,' Nance would say. 'Isn't a duty on us all
to carry our own crosses! God of Glory will shine the light
amongst us yet. Tim will come home! Something is telling
me he will.'

'I don't think, Nance, my treasure, that I'll ever hear
again from him. That night I told him to have no more
to do with you, up or down, he got in a passion. He didn't
say "That's bad, mother," only dashed up to the room. In
the morning he wasn't rising and I thought he was cross.

When I thought it long that he wasn't rising, I went up, but the bed was cold empty, and looking as though nobody had lain on it. The little window was unmoved. I looked around the room. Nothing was moved only his holiday clothes—there wasn't a tatter of them to be found. Nance, my treasure, that's the time the grip caught me. I called Tim but nobody heeded me. Kate, down here, was the first person who came and when she heard the story she started to sing her wailing. The whole hamlet was around us inside half an hour. I was brought in between people without my mind or anybody else's mind. When any glimpse of my mind came back to me, you were the first person I saw, with a cup of water in your hand.'

'I was, surely,' said Nance. 'The other people panicked and nobody stayed with you only myself. I thought there wasn't a scrap of truth in it. I wouldn't let it into my mind that there was. God wouldn't do me such a wrong—I was too fond of Tim. If Tim was dead as many others believe, I wouldn't live. I'd play the hanging trick! But I say again that there's something telling me he'll return!'

'But, Nance, it's well you know he doesn't live, only you consoling me. Tim is as dead as a stone—'

'Listen! What's this, Betty? There's somebody coming.'

'Who would be coming at this hour of the night? It was the wind did it.'

'I suppose so,' said Nance. 'But I hear it again—somebody is coming!'

'It's the wind shaking the trees, Nance. It's often before this the same noise startled me. I'd swear somebody would be coming, but that person never came.'

'By my word, Betty, but I have sharper ears than that. I hear the person's footfall, he is there and he is coming up the path to the house. He'll be here immediately whoever he is.'

A knock comes to the door. Nance hops to the door and takes the bolt off it. A slender dark man puts his head in and the water falling in drops down on his face from the cap on his head.

'It's not Tim,' said Nance, in her own mind, and that thought brought a sigh out of her heart.

'God's blessing in here,' said the stranger.

Nance draws back.

'Who are you, please?' said she, and she looked at him inquisitively between the two eyes.

'I am a man in the King's service,' said he. ''Tis how I was sent here with a message, a letter I have here that was found in a bottle that was floating with the tide. I was told to take it to this woman. The guards said it was her son wrote it a couple of years ago.'

'And where did they get the bottle that that letter was in, good man?' said Nance.

'It's hard to say. Some sea-faring people picked it up, I suppose.'

'You are a good messenger,' said Nance. 'See now, Betty, what did I tell you?'

'What's that man saying, Nance? I don't understand a word from him. You have English, tell me what he says.'

'He has good news. A letter from Tim he brought to us.'

'A letter from Tim! What's that you're saying?'

'He says it was in a bottle the letter was found and that it was your son Tim who wrote it, a couple of years ago.'

'Oh! I don't know will I believe my ears,' said she. 'Is this a dream or can it come true?' and she thought to get out on the fence and sing that lonesome dirge. But Nance turned her away and put her sitting on the little stool in the corner.

'Have sense,' she said, 'God's help is nearer than the door.'

'Oh! Nance, make attendance on this good man who brought us the good news! Hang the kettle quickly and make a cup of tea for him.'

Then Nance hung the kettle and it wasn't long until the tea was ready. The wanderer drank a couple of cups of tea, for he had need of it. Then he went out.

Nance opened the letter and read it aloud, because Betty was a little bit deaf.

'Dear Mother, you did me wrong,' she read. 'If you saw the hardship I'm in you'd never forgive yourself. But it's hard to say that this letter will ever reach you. I am here now in a small boat and no ground or land within forty miles of me. I have nothing to see in any direction I look but the sea and the brilliant stars above me. The ship sank and we had to take to the boats. I didn't think, Mother, when I left you, that such disaster would catch me. This morning a man of our team died and we had to throw him overboard. There are now only six of us and even one of those is failing. There is nothing threatening us more than the thirst. The captain is entreating us not to dare drink the brine. He says we are near the hot countries, but 'tis how the poor man is giving us courage. If this letter reaches you, Mother, I am asking one thing of you, before I'm swallowed to the bottom, to be fond of poor Nance for my sake. This is like a letter from the grave, dear Mother, but there's only one chance in a thousand that it will reach you, but I'll meet you again among the dead, with God's help.

I am your fond son,

Tim.'

'Read it again, Nance,' said Betty. 'I like fine to be listening to you reading it.'

Nance read the letter again.

'Yes, Betty,' said she, 'I told you Tim wasn't after dying!'

'Musha, Nance, my pet, I have little delusion but that the poor man is on the way of eternity long ago.'

'He's not at all; 'tis how the little boat was thrown in on some shore far from home. Maybe 'tis how Tim was exhausted and he's in some hospital in faraway places. Have your hope in God! That letter gave me great courage. We'll have better news before long. Go to sleep now and sleep soundly. Tim is out of danger. I'll go home.'

'Whisper,' said Betty, 'don't stay away from me at all, but come and visit me always.'

'Don't be afraid,' said Nance, and she went.

Time was slipping by and the friendship between Betty and Nance was growing. People wondered at the love the two always had for each other, but that was a secret between the two themselves. But it was said that whatever trick Nance had played on Betty she was going to present the little farm to her and any young man she'd lay her eye on. But poor Nance's eye was west over the wild seas always and for ever until the day the gathering was at the crossroad.

All the people of the parish were there and because they were, Kate Jim urged me along with her. When we went west, Betty was standing amongst the people as grey as a mouse and Nance standing beside her looking very confused. Tim Betty was a pillar of a nobleman, not speaking a word of Gaelic. Myself and Kate Jim went up to Betty's house and we had a great day. Soon after that Tim and Nance were married.

Nance was right when she told Betty that Tim was out of danger. What Tim himself said was that it was likely that Nance got the award for her prayer. 'Because,' he said, 'approaching the banks of Newfoundland, the greatest squall of wind I ever saw came upon us. The sea increased and swelled until the ghost of a big mountain was in every

green-sided wave of it. The waves were beating so strongly
on our ship that the cargo shifted in her. A little boy ran
into the cabin where I was and the fear of death on him.
"Oh! God with my soul!" said he, "the ship is in small
bits. The water is coming up through the floor of the ship.
She'll go under! She'll go under!" said he and he went.
I didn't understand at first, however, what sense the little
boy had with the talk, but it was shortly after that I found
out. Because I was only settled in the little boat when the
big ship was swallowed down before our sight.

'We stayed that night being thrown from wave to wave
and in the morning there was no boat or ship to be seen,
that would come in any aid to us. The only hope we had
then was that maybe in the granting of God, some ship
would come the way that would pick us up and out of
our predicament. But it was the spit for the venison and
the deer not yet killed. On the third morning there was a
man of our team failing. "Oh!" said he, "If I can't quench
my thirst I'll die! My tongue is withered in my head," and
he bent down and drank the brine. But if he did, the brine
killed him. Then the captain told us not to drink the brine
any more, however we'd fare. On the morning of the fourth
day we hadn't ground or land to see. Another man of our
team shouted and said that he was finished; "I couldn't put
up with it," said he, and he gave one jump out into the sea.
He sent the brine in splashes in the sky. He spent a little
while struggling in the water and then he went down.

'As the sun was setting that evening I felt my strength
failing me. There was some weakness coming on my heart.
I knew my time was spent, but before I fell I heard the
captain saying there was some land near us, where the
lights were clearly to be seen, but I remembered no more.
When I came to myself again, where I was was in the big
hospital in Buenos Aires. I must admit that the captain did

a noble deed for me, may God repay him for his toil! He put a good nurse attending to me. And only for the good attention I got, I suppose I wouldn't be alive today. It wasn't long until I was able to walk in and out for myself again. One day when I was going to work who should I meet but a lad from Dingle. We got acquainted. He told me all that had happened since I left Ireland. He told me about the friendship between you and Nance, and that you were going to present the small farm to her and any man she'd lay her eye on. When I heard him say that much, I admit it moved me greatly. I said to myself that nobody would have Nance as long as strength and pluck would be in my limbs, that I would go and earn enough to bring me home to Ireland, and when everything was ready, I travelled and I came to rest here, myself and Nance.'

'Musha, may God award the luck down on yourself and Nance!' said Betty. 'Soon I'll be leaving ye, but I'll die happily now seeing you both together again.'

It was soon after that Betty was called from this life, but many a merry evening myself and Kate Jim had with Nance McDonagh afterwards.

CHAPTER TEN

Wethers' Well Pilgrimage; a Pagan and the Wethers; the Overcoat

'Would you go on the pilgrimage, Peig?' said Big Kate to me one evening in the end of June, as I was going to the well to fetch a bucket of water.

'What pilgrimage, Kate?' said I.

'Wethers' Well pilgrimage,' said she. 'A lot of the people of the island are going there and we'll have great company.'

'Och, my grief,' said I, 'that place is too far from home.'

'It's not, indeed,' said Kate. 'Don't people go farther from home than it? I was there long ago when I was a little girl, with my mother, and I have decided to go there this year and I'd like you to be along with me. One person is no good, but a pair is company.'

'Indeed, I'd love to be with ye, and I will, with God's help, if possible,' said I. A couple of days after that I met her again.

'Musha, Kate, since they're all going there, I won't break the company; I'll go with you. But when will ye be going there?'

'St. Peter and Paul Day is the right day for the pilgrimage, but we would have to be in Dingle the night before because the train will be going early. Be ready in the morning,' said she.

'All right,' said I, 'it's a day of my life, nobody knows who'll live,' and I went to fetch the water.

Tomorrow morning many of the people of the island were preparing themselves for the road. When I was ready

I made down for the shore. There was noise there before, before me, oars and canoes being put down, a man with the thole-pins, another man with the oars, and another man with a little white bag on his back. And what a din they had! There were eighteen persons of us going on the pilgrimage. I myself was in the canoe when Kate came. She made a fine wide shout of a musical laugh up from the bottom of her heart when she saw the driving that they had.

'By my baptism, men,' said she, 'but we're busy, it seems. We'll not be lonely, with the help of God, certainly.'

The sea was fine and quiet and the canoes were besting each other. The sea was broken by the eternal dipping of the oars. There was a path of white foam after them. You'd hear now and again a boasting shout from a man when a canoe would creep up a little by another.

'Indeed,' said Kate to myself, 'a person would think there was a big bet down, so hard they are going—or why all the contending?'

'Oh! did you never hear, Kate, that Youth is mad?' said I. 'They have the youth and the courage and the great humour that's on them is urging them. They are decided to have the day of sport, because it's not always the lads of the island have a day like that.'

'On my soul,' said Kate, 'but the old people are merrier than them. Don't you see how airy Michael is! His heart is as light as a thrush.'

'It is, and there's nobody in the company heartier than he,' said I.

'This is a wonderful charge of rowing,' said Big Owen.

'Arragh! listen, man, she was never driven so since a nail was hammered into her,' said Sean Owen, 'but she'd do as much again if those two delaying women weren't in her.'

'You'll show the effect of it, Sean,' said Kate, 'you won't be thirsty when we get to Dingle.'

'On my soul, but that's ever your nature, Kate!' said Sean, and he bent his oars.

I was looking west from me at Grey Top at that time, and at the Blaskets. The air was so blue over me that you'd think it had just been painted by some painter. The brown heather was on the top of the peaks west from me between me and the bottom of the sky and over and hither there was a small patch of green to be seen, the small steady houses on the edge of the cliff and a little barren hill-crest above them. Its golden summit was as a shelter from the threatening wind that blows across the gap.

Anyone who would be where I was that day and who would look into life, he would have something to think about. He would have compassion for the poor people who are living on such a stump from the sea, trying to make a living there. But I hadn't much of my life spent yet. Less had I much understanding of life and there was nothing to be done but to take the easy end of the matter.

'Wouldn't you be talking, Peig?' said Kate. 'What are you thinking about?'

'That lovely view that's before me I am seeing,' said I. 'Isn't it a fine thing to be on the sea on a calm day!'

'You are right, Peig,' said Big Owen, 'it's a fine thing to be on the sea, but the small of your back not to be paying for it.'

'And as we know, Owen,' said I, 'all the hurry wasn't needed. Wouldn't ye take it easy? Don't you know that the women have their own duties? Is it how you'd think to put us rowing?'

'I leave in my will to God that there was never much good in your likes only the talk you have! Do you hear this, Kate?'

When we went to Cliff Top, there was a party of us there and we were all talking and listening to each other as is usual with the people of the island. At last Sean Owen spoke out loud.

'What misfortune is keeping ye there? Isn't there a long road ahead of us yet? Isn't it many a step from here to Dingle?'

'It's many, musha, Sean,' said Big Kate, answering him, 'and there won't be much liveliness in the women when we reach the place, below.'

'There's a great fear of ye,' said Owen. 'It's a long time before this since much walking was got from your legs.'

Kate stretched herself and tightened her shawl around her. If she was middle-aged itself, she was nice and hard.

'Come on over east,' said she to me. 'Mary Keating will make a cup of tea for us, and it will do us good for the road.'

'Here it's with you,' said I.

When we came into Mary's house, you'd think it was down from the sky we had fallen to her.

'Going on the pilgrimage ye are, I suppose,' said she.

'Yes, musha,' said Kate, 'it's how we came over here so that you'd make a cup of tea for us if you don't mind.'

'I don't, certainly,' said Mary. 'The kettle is boiling and you won't have much delay.'

We had the tea only just on the table when Sean Owen came in the door.

'Out of your bodies be it,' said Sean, 'if it's not good to yourselves you are!'

'Don't be talking,' said Kate, 'but sit here and have your own mouth's desire of it.'

'He may as well,' said Mary, 'it's the same thanks he'll get.'

'Musha,' said Sean, 'what goes on, runs. I may as well have a drop of it. The same tea is a wonderful herb.'

'Sean, my pet,' said Mary, 'didn't you hear that the Lord God long ago said that an herb would grow through the ground and that that herb would be more in the mouths of people than Himself?'

'Praise for ever to His glorious name!' said Sean, and he took his hat off his head. 'But, Mary, what about the tobacco?'

'Musha, the way the matter is, Sean, is that the people are worn away to the bone for it. But you'd get a person who'd refuse tobacco, but there's nobody alive would turn the back of his hand to a cup of tea.'

'On my speckled oath, but you've beaten me again,' said Sean. 'But if your appetite for tea is as great as mine for tobacco, I don't rely on your luck.'

'The King of Powers knows, my pet, that it's together I prefer them,' said Mary.

'Yes, this won't do,' said Sean. 'Women, it's as well for us to be moving,' and he put an ember of fire on his pipe and we went out together. The rest of the people of the island were out the Hollows before us but we caught up with them on the long road down, and I'm telling you that we weren't lonely as long as Sean Owen was with us. He was a fine chatty man, and a good man, too.

Joseph O'Shea's house was the first tavern we met.

'In here with ye, men,' said Big Kate, 'I promised Sean Owen this morning that he'd have a drink when he'd reach Dingle and I may as well fulfil my promise, but 'tis no work to make flesh of one person and fish of another.'

'My soul, Kate,' said Owen, 'but there's high fussing on you, but the big heart must have its way.'

It was a sister of Kate's was married to Owen, and that made them very great with each other.

'It's as well to obey her,' said Sean, 'there's no use giving her a refusal.'

'Indeed,' said Michael, 'but ye are more inclined to go in than ye will be to come out, but as it's a thing that's said,

"A house by the roadside is not a journey, but a short-cut", here it is with ye.'

In with us and we sat at a table that was in the room. Big Kate came with a gallon of porter—it was easy to buy a gallon of porter at that time. She put it down in front of Sean Owen on the table.

'Share that out to the company, Sean,' said she, 'for the goose's beak is not longer than the gander's. Everyone in this company is dear to me.'

'Will you have a drop, yourself, Kate?' said Sean.

'I won't, my treasure,' said she. 'The women prefer the hot drop. Myself and Peig will have a half-glass.'

We drank the half-glass, and then myself and Kate went out. It was late enough then and we had to get our lodgings for the night.

'Where will we go, Kate?' said I.

'We'll go east to the carpenter's house,' said she, 'because it's there I stay every night I'm in Dingle.'

We went east and when we went in Brigid, the woman of the house, was standing in the shop, and she put a hundred welcomes before us.

'You have arrived from west,' said she. 'Did more of ye come?'

'There did, by my soul,' said Kate, 'and a party.'

'For the pilgrimage, I suppose?' said Brigid.

'Oh! Yes! what else?' said Kate 'We're tired out from the road. Come on in to the kitchen,' said she to myself.

We went back to the kitchen and Brigid followed us.

'Throw off your shawls! I suppose it's nowhere else you'll go tonight again?' said Brigid.

'Musha, no. Our feet are blistered with the road,' said Kate.

'I suppose so, my pet,' said Brigid, and she went from us out to the shop.

We weren't long sitting when a middle-aged woman came down the stair and came into the kitchen.

'Welcome, women of the island!' said she.

'May you live long, Joan,' said Kate, 'how are you spending life these times?'

'Musha, weak, sound and thin,' said Joan. 'It's not improving but failing we'll be each day. Age creeps up on everyone, and it's not always a person can be as he wishes.'

She drew to her a little stool by the fire.

'On my soul,' said Kate, 'you have it nicely.'

'This is my own stool. I don't be looking for a seat from anybody,' said she.

'It's a proverb,' said Kate, ' "If you go to a wedding uninvited, bring with you a stool to sit on"!'

'That's just how it is with me,' said Joan. ''Tis how I have a while here and a while there and wherever I stay I bring my stool with me.'

'Musha, a cause to laugh for us!' said Kate, 'Tim of Dingle is in a hundred places.'

Joan was a countrywoman and she had to leave her own house because she and her son's wife didn't agree together. She had pence of money, and she was paying for a small room in the carpenter's house. She was a nice chatty woman and many a thing she talked about.

She wasn't long sitting when she produced her white clay pipe and started to put tobacco in it.

'Do you smoke tobacco, island woman?' said she to Kate.

'Musha, my pet, great is my appetite for it,' said Kate, 'but with the contending I had on me this morning I forgot my pipe at home. But as we know, I have no excuse now. Can't I get them, both tobacco and pipe here?'

'Yes, definitely,' said Joan, 'you'll want for nothing here if you have money in your pocket, but if you haven't got that you'll be often short,' and she reached her pipe to

Kate; and on my soul it was the hiding in the fool's hand the pipe being given to Kate, because she took smoke out of it. After a little while I asked Joan a question.

'Do you know, old woman, with what saint or woman saint is the Wethers' Well pilgrimage connected?'

'Musha, certainly, that's a thing I don't know, but I'll tell you what I heard about it. 'Tis how there was a goodly rich man living in that place. He was a pagan, and he had good tract of land, but he wanted to protect the field the pilgrimage is in now for meadow. He had a protecting fence around the field so that no animal could cross, but he noticed the field was being bared and the grass being eaten. He became suspicious of his servant boy, that he was giving the grazing of the field to someone else, unknown to him. He questioned the boy but the boy gave denial in the matter. He said he had nothing to do with anything of the sort. "All right," said the pagan, "the field must be watched. Something is baring the grass. You'll have to go and watch the field tonight, and you'll know what's doing it." "All right," said the boy.

'When the night came the poor boy went and settled himself in the corner of the field. He wasn't long there when he heard the grass being pulled and some animals grazing, but he couldn't see anything. He'd think he should see something, but he didn't. He walked all around the field. He'd hear the noise but he couldn't see anything. On to-morrow's morning he told the master what happened to him the night before. "You fool," said the master, "I knew it was a wrong to trust in you doing watching like that. But I won't be depending on you, I'll go there myself tonight." "All right," said the boy, "the fox never sent anyone better than himself out. Maybe you'll succeed in seeing things better than I did."

'The night that was coming, the pagan took with him in

his hand a hard blackthorn stick and called the boy with him. When they reached the field, one of them went into hiding in the bottom of the field and other at the top. In the dead time of night the eating started near the place where the pagan was in hiding. He leapt out from the side of the fence, to find out what was eating the grass. He saw the three white wethers in their wool, he thought. Here he goes after them. They did the round of the field but he couldn't catch up with them. He shouted out loud to the boy to come and help him, but the boy couldn't see a sheep or a wether or a lamb. The master was cornering them ever and forever until he had them in the middle of the field and he thought they were tired out, and he gave a running charge to catch one of them. But he didn't succeed, because the three wethers put down their heads and went down through the ground in front of his two eyes. As we know panic and terror came on him, and he moved over to where they disappeared from his sight. He could see no trace of them, but he could see another thing, that is the spring well and the three round stones like stones of the shore, settled around the well. He became terrified and he called the boy. "Did you see anything?" said the master when the boy came to him. "I didn't see anything only yourself going around the field, and 'tis how I thought you had left your senses. Was it something you saw yourself?" "Yes, certainly," said the master, "and as you're a Christian can you give me any explanation for what I saw tonight?" Then he started to tell the boy what he saw and how the wethers went down through the ground when he threw the stick he had in his hand at them. "And now," said he, "I have no trace of it to see only that waterwell that wasn't there before." "It's a wonderful thing," said the boy, "but it's our parish priest would best explain it to you." "All right, boy. Come on home, we'll have enough time to think in the morning." Next day he sent the boy to the priest to tell him the story. When the priest heard that story from the boy he told him to tell his master that he'd like to have a little talk with him.

'The pagan had no hesitation, because what he had seen put great fear on him. The end of the story was,' said Joan, 'that the priest baptized the pagan and his household at the well. The Church blessed the place after that. On St. Peter and Paul day they were baptized and the pilgrimage was consecrated for that day, and the big crowds from far and near are making the pilgrimage ever since, and that's why, my pet, it's called the pilgrimage of Wethers' Well.'

Next morning, at dawn of day, we were up and everyone at his best to reach the station. O person of my heart, there were some of us who never saw a train before and we made great wonder of it. There were a lot of people gathered there, because the train wasn't going yet. They were from north and south there. The people of the island would like to be in one carriage, because where one of them would like to be was where the others would like to be. We were standing near the train, and pooling our advice. It was Big Owen O'Sullivan[1] was our leader. He was a fine well-standing man that day.

'We didn't need all the hurry, men,' said Sean. 'I don't know how long more we'll be here?'

'Not long,' said a man from Dingle. 'You must be going in, because the train will be going in a couple of minutes.'

In with us on the train, and we seated ourselves. There were a lot of people with us in it. We barely had room on the seats.

When we reached Tralee station the train stopped. A man came to us for tickets and as he'd get a ticket he'd cut a small gap out of it, and give it back to us.

[1] 'Grandfather' in Maurice O'Sullivan's book. See *Twenty Years a-Growing*.

We went together out of the train.

'Yes, men,' said Sean Owen, cleaning the dust of the carriage from his clothes, 'what's to be done?'

'What's to be done only to be packing ahead?' said Michael. 'Haven't we the width of our feet of the dry land of Ireland. If we're going west awhile we haven't but to turn and then take the other way; the day is long and it's with ourselves we'll be spending it.'

'If I had drunk a couple pints of porter,' said Big Owen, 'I wouldn't mind whether 'twould be east or west we'd be going.'

'Come with me,' said Big Kate, 'I know Mary Brosnahan, she's an old friend of mine, since she used to stay in Dingle. I don't know what part of the Town she's in, but if I found somebody who would direct us to the house . . .'

At that, a little boy came the way and I spoke to him in broken English, and asked him, if it were his will, to show us Kate Brosnahan's house.

'It is,' said he, and he went down the street before us. When we reached the house, Owen put his hand in his pocket and gave a sixpence to the little boy for sweets.

As soon as the woman of the house saw Big Kate she put hundreds of welcomes before her, and before us all because she had the best of acquaintance with a good many people of the island.

'Be seated! Ye'll have a good drink, I suppose,' said she.

'We will, but we have no business in being slow,' said Owen, 'because we'll have to be ready for the train this evening, and if you could arrange any coach that would take us to the pilgrimage, we'd have plenty of time.'

'I can, certainly,' said she. 'I have one of them myself that will take ye out and back together.'

'Thank you, woman of the house, the matter is right, then,' said Owen.

It was a long coach, a two-horse coach. We sat in, nine on each side.

'My soul from the Devil,' said Sean, 'but we're having a great time, if the end of it is not looking for charity.'

'If it is itself, it's merry work,' said Michael, answering him.

'Dear men,' said Owen, 'we'll be only a time in this life, and don't ye know that it's your folly if you don't borrow from it.'

'Arrah! Owen, it's not today this gayness will be regretted, but when we'll go home.'

'Listen, you fool,' said Michael, and his hat raised up, 'you'll be dead and nobody will say God's blessing with your soul. Cast it up to yourself, man. A day will come on you and on me when we won't be able to come on Wethers' Well Pilgrimage.'

'I suppose you're right, Michael,' said Sean, and he started to put tobacco in his pipe.

It wasn't long until we reached the pilgrimage field. The crowds were there, a party coming and a party going. I myself didn't forget the little story that Joan was telling us last night before that, because I noticed everything around the field and especially the well and the wethers, as they say. I thought in my mind that many lives had gone since the pagan was there.

As soon as we had finished the pilgrimage, we hopped into the coach and while you'd be saying 'one, two, three', we were at the inn. There was food ready there before us and people in waiting busy, because it was not only the people of the island who were eating there that day. There was a long roomy table in the middle of the room and seats around it, and as for other things that have to do with dinner, they were on the table.

We were eating and talking, because we were hungry enough, but the bread was eaten and we weren't half-satisfied.

'On my baptism,' said Sean, 'the bread is eaten and we haven't half enough.'

'Speak to the girl, Sean, and tell her to bring us more bread,' said Michael.

But though he did, 'twas small heed the girl paid him. She didn't know but it was Latin he spoke. 'Tis how she giggled and went away. But the girl wasn't coming and we were waiting. She was busy waiting on other people. They had Nonie down and Nonie up and she answering them at her best. At last Thomas stood up and spoke aloud: 'MORE BREAD, NONIE,' said he. In a minute she was to us with an armful of bread.

'Yes, Sean, is the English good?' said Thomas. 'If you knew that much we wouldn't be waiting so long.'

'On my speckled oath,' said Sean, 'but you have me hit in the eye.'

'Did ye ever hear,' said Owen, 'that the ebbtide waits not for noon, and no less than that will the train wait for us. This is not the Island ye have, where the canoe will wait for ye until ye are ready.'

That made us anxious and everyone was at his best to get to the station. When we reached it you'd think nobody ever died, there were so many people there. Every carriage was full.

'Come into this carriage,' said Kate, 'we surely must find room somewhere.' When we went in a wren wouldn't find room on any of the seats, but there was a place where an overcoat was stretched the length of the seat.

'What about the overcoat, Kate,' said I, 'isn't there room for three under it?'

'I don't know in life, my treasure,' said she, 'I suppose it's somebody put it there to keep room.'

'If so, musha,' said I, 'it will keep only his own place, whoever it belongs to.'

I caught the overcoat and I folded it and I planked it down on the seat with so much room under it that if it was the devil himself he'd have enough room. Then Kate and I sat on what was left of the seat. We were squashed enough but it was better than to be standing. But after a couple of minutes two men came into the box. One of them was a nice middle-aged man from Dingle and the other a big fat strong man who had a basketful of a stomach. A watch in his pocket and a yellow chain across and the appearance on him that he was a fine gentleman. He stood in front of us and asked in English who folded his overcoat like that. Nobody answered him. Then the Dingle man spoke in Gaelic and asked who moved this good man's coat.

' 'Twas I moved it, good man,' said I.

'Where did you find it in yourself to do the like?' said he, and anger in his voice.

'Because I understood the overcoat to belong to one person and that by right it deserved only one man's space, and if you haven't your entitled space, righteous man, I will leave this place to you. Though there's good bulk in you, I think you have enough room, because I have bought this seat as well as you. There was no bad penny in my money when I paid for it.'

'Didn't you always hear,' said the Dingle man to the fat hulk, 'that nobody ever got the better of women?'

'I did,' said the big man, 'and it's true.'

'Sit here on my knee,' said the Dingle man, 'we'll have every second turn.'

There was no more talk about the overcoat, but that didn't leave us without company because Michael and more of the people of the island were at one end of the carriage, his hat on his knee, singing. 'Dark Woman's Slope', he was at, and he taking an echo out of the carriage. I was looking out through the window at the little hamlets and green plains, for it was my first time ever on a train—and the last, because I was never on a train since.

I noticed the little hamlets and at the same time giving ear to Michael who was in a merry mood at the head of the carriage. Over and hither, there would be people in the fields. Whatever they were doing, you'd think the train would startle them because you'd see the fine healthy red faces, and the sign of sustenance on them, looking in at you through the windows of the train; but before there'd be a clear sight of them you'd be rushed away again like the wind. There was nothing ever resembled them but cormorants bobbing up after shooting at them.

It wasn't long until the man of the overcoat had enough room. As the train was moving west a person was leaving it until we reached Dingle. Everyone was busy then getting to his own house. We had little delay to make in Dingle and as the evening was fine and the sea calm we did our best to get home. It was a lovely night, the air was clean, full of brilliant stars and the moon shining on the sea. From time to time a sea-bird would give a cry. Inside in the black caves where the moon was not shining the seals were lamenting to themselves. I would hear, too, the murmuring of the sea running in and out through the clefts of the stones and the music of the oars cleaving the sea across to Ventry.

'My soul from the devil,' said Sean Owen, and he put so much strength into that much speech, that he startled me, 'is there anyone here who will sing up my praise-song?'

'I am here,' said Michael, and he started to sing the words:

'Did ye hear account of the nice BEAUTY of the island?
She drew fame with a crew of good men on the shore;
When they were let go on the long course of the shore
They were in the evening as exhausted as race-horses.'

And he continued long, soft and sweet. When the crew of the other canoe that was a small distance in front of us heard him, they didn't let it go to him. They were into competition and nobody knew who was the best howler. The proverb says, and it's true, that a good story-bringer in a house is no better than a bad one. But it's not over my saying it, Michael was the sweetest singer I ever heard. When he had the song sung, Sean Owen drew up a snipe of a bottle from a little white bag that was near him. 'Here, son of a good mother, quench your thirst with this,' said he. Michael caught the bottle and took a flowing drink from it. The bottle was not put by. Before it parted with them there wasn't a drop in the bottom of it. It's out in the sea Sean Owen threw it.

We weren't long coming home, and it was for long after that there was remembrance of the Wethers' Well Pilgrimage.

CHAPTER ELEVEN

How the Fish was Stolen from Old Kate and how Herself ate some of it

A couple of days after the Pilgrimage I met my man, Sean Owen.

'My soul from the devil,' said he to me, 'wasn't it I acted the rake that day! I spent all I had in the world, woman of my heart, and the mistress is mad with me since. She didn't even speak a kind word to me. 'Tis how she does have a wallop at the cat and a wallop at the dog. She has me in the goat's horns. Whatever pricked me to go to the same pilgrimage I didn't bring much of the grace of God home with me! I'm telling you, little woman, that it was the unfortunate pilgrimage for me. If everybody who was on the pilgrimage is being persecuted as I am they won't feel like going on Wethers' Well pilgrimage ever again.'

'Musha, Sean, you have only to give them the deaf ear. That much will go in the sky with the wind, and it's a good thing the money was in your pocket. Didn't you ever hear that a big-hearted man in a big town is a pity without money in his pocket? You are not a played-out man yet. But you remind me of a fine spring evening long ago when I was listening to Nora Paddy. She had the same grousing at her husband, James Patrick. He was after coming home from Dingle, and he had drunk a drop—and by the way a woman's tongue is a thing that doesn't rust. He got the tongue from Nora, and got it black, because he had brought her no piece of sauce for the Fitzgerald who was coming to plough for them the next day. She had him tormented with eternal grumbling.

' "In the name of God, woman," said James, "stop now! As we know, I never remembered that you or the Fitzgerald were alive. But go you west to Old Kate and you'll get a couple of fish to borrow from her."

' "On my soul," said Nora, "but 'tis sooner Old Kate would part with the eye, than with any fish. Fish is scarce and the poor creature herself has only a little."

' "And aren't there two tellings on every story and two sides on every page?" said he. "Wouldn't you try the crow's trick on her? If you can do it anyhow, we'll have a chance to repay her, please God."

' "On my soul, James," said Nora, "isn't it harder to steal her temple from the wasp than sneak up on Old Kate to take any fish from her. She is watching them like the cat would be watching the mouse. I don't think the grey crow himself could trick her. But I'll have a try at her anyway."

'Old Kate was sitting by the fence sunning a small lot of fish on the fence, and if her hut went on fire she wouldn't leave the fence, for watching the fish, and it would be hard for anyone to come near it unknown to her. But well as she was watching, Nora got a chance on her. She sneaked down into the bottom of the garden which was full of bushes and jungle so that a person would think the cat itself couldn't pass among them. She slid on up to the fence and put her hand up where the fish was, and swiped three fishes without Old Kate seeing her. Then she slid away the same way like an eel.

'When she came to the house, with the fish, James was there.

' "By my palms," said he, "but there are people as bad as Frawley[1] alive! That's the quickest theft anyone ever did! But Old Kate will have to be repaid!"

[1] A famous robber.

' "It's a small danger that I'd have anything of Old Kate's, only I was in a spot. I wouldn't like the Fitzgerald to have unflavoured food. A person has a desire for fish in the spring."

'When Old Kate arose and looked around her, she noticed that three small fishes were gone without trace. Then it was that she had the history and the cursing.

' "Breaking and bruising of bones on the one who took them!" said she, but many a laugh she had afterwards when Nora was telling her about the scraping and scratching she got among the bushes trying to take them with her.'

'I wonder did she tell her it was herself took them?' said Sean.

'She did, without doubt,' said I. 'This is how it happened. About dinner-time, she went in to Nora and they had the food just on the table. She saluted them.

' "God and Mary to you, old woman," said Nora. "Food-time is a good time."

' "It is, indeed," said Kate. "It's better for everyone to have something than all to be without."

' "Sit now, old woman, until I warm a drop of milk for you. You like the milk."

' "I do, my treasure," said Old Kate.

'Nora passed her the warm milk and a couple of potatoes and a scrap of fish.

' "Musha, may God not prevent your hand from sharing, O daughter!" said she.

' "Did you hear what the robber said to the poor man long ago, when he gave him the meat to eat?" said Nora.

' "I didn't, my pet. What did he say?" said Old Kate.

' "'Tis how he had a couple of beasts stolen from him by the same rogue and it happened that he came the way to the robber's house one night unexpectedly—and that was the generous, welcoming house! Meat was passed to him in plenty, but the poor man was timid. Although he had a good desire for the meat, he didn't want to be a glutton. The robber spoke to him.

' " 'Eat the food, poor man!' said he. 'Eat your fill of the cows of Grey John of Cow-herb!'

' "When the poor man heard that, it wounded him to the heart, because he was Grey John himself, and he couldn't eat another bite, but he pretended he was very grateful to them. He had the very opposite under the rib, because he had the robber arrested the following night. And it's the same way with you and me, Kate," said Nora. "You eat your fill of your own, too, because 'tis I took the fish from you unknown to you."

' "Musha, a cause to laugh for us!" said Old Kate, "I thought by the watching I had that neither crow nor eagle could come near to it unknown to me!"

' "I was afraid," said Nora, "that if I asked you for it you'd be reluctant to give it to me. I made out that I'd come from north-west on you."

' "I suppose I would, too," said Old Kate, "but the matter is right now. Haven't I my own share of it?" '

'There's no stop on a person when he thinks of doing a trick like that,' said Sean. 'But I have the day spent, and the work undone. When will I be back from the Wide Peak with a load of turf?'

'The day is long yet,' said I. 'A good man's turn of it is yet to be spent.'

'You're right,' said Sean, but he hit the black ass a lick of the stick he had in his hand, and drove on. The poor ass was slow and lazy, and I think the delay I was putting on Sean was doing him good. The poor animal was startled when he felt the hard stick brought to bear on his ribs. He shook his untidy ears and moved forward quickly. He was obedient to his master, for it's often the master was not too gentle with the creature. Wasn't it he knew the angry master?—and to tell the truth it wasn't the gentle acquaintance, because it was on him he'd work off all his crossness.

I was alone again, looking around me, and Sean as far as my shout up the road and he taking dust out of the black ass. I'd hear now and again the sound of his voice. 'Tis how the ass was lazy, for the day was very hot, and I don't think my man was very satisfied in his mind the same day. The Wethers' Well pilgrimage was a subject for thought with him yet.

CHAPTER TWELVE

An Ass, a Bag of Potatoes, and Geese; Mackerel Shoaling

What I am thinking about now, sitting here, is that life has changed greatly compared with twenty years ago. At that time the people of the island had rummaging and hauling, and especially when the mackerel season was in.

There's a little harbour down the cliff, and it's not a very good harbour. The boot-marks of the unfortunates are to be seen on the grey stones of the beach. They have a track cut in the stone from being down and up there, and to top every hardship, there's danger of drowning there.

I see the picture of the unfortunates before me. I see the shape of them, and his own bundle on each man's back, going down to the harbour. I hear, I think, the noise of the canoes being laid on the slip and the nets being drawn into them. A little while after that I see the canoes steering out into the mouth of the creek and the people talking to each other. The mackerel are shoaling in big patches out west on the waters of the shore, but there's too much day left for the fisherman to stretch out his nets. He is waiting until the stars shine in the sky. Look, there's a boat east and a boat west already. They are scattered like the small birds. The oars make noise, beating the water and splashing it in white foam in the sky, trying to race each other. At the same time I see the old women fussily running west at the top of the shore. They wouldn't break a hen-egg under their feet, the heart is so high up in their breasts, and they wouldn't wait to take the cups off the table, they're in such bodily haste.

I remember well a fine harvest evening like that. The lateness of evening was there, and the canoes gone out fishing. I had a ridge of potatoes ungathered and I had to go and gather them. I took a couple of little bags on the back of an old white ass I had and west to the Mouth of the Shore—a little garden we had at the edge of the shore and we called it that because it was so near to the White Shore. My head was down, picking at my best, when I heard all the uproar and chatter west beyond me. I lifted my head and looked around me, but I saw nothing only the little children of the hamlet taking the heels off each other running towards the top of the shore. I made out there was something wonderful there, but whatever it was I had no sight of it, for I was in a hollow. When I had picked all, and the bags were full, I couldn't put them on the ass's back, because they were too heavy. I was waiting there until somebody would come the way who would help me to lift them up. It wasn't the long wait I had, because Sean Michael came to me from east, and I asked him to put the bags on the ass's back with me. It was short delay on him to put the bags on the ass's back without much help from me.

'Drive him with you now,' said he, 'and I'll close the gate.'

I drove on, the road east, but the uproar was still there, and I could see nothing of what was going on. But I wasn't far east when two women met me with soldierly stance, at a sharp speed. They hardly spoke to me, they were so anxious.

'God of powers, where are ye going, that so much striving is on ye?' said I. 'Or what's going on west?'

'There isn't a drop of water on Yellow Island shore only mackerel shoaling!' said Nell, 'and all the canoes are in a way to sink each other around them,' and she went from me, in a hurry. They were of no importance only there was another couple after them and another couple and the same hurry on them. My heart was to be among them, but as we know, how could I because of having the potatoes on the ass's back? If I left him there it would be the fox in charge of the hens with me because the devil a one of them but he'd have eaten when I'd return. Therefore I had nothing to do only take it easy and press home. On the way before me was Pat Mickey, the blessing of God with his soul, standing at the fence and a spade under his chest.

'By my oath, Pat Mickey, but the women of the hamlet are off their head tonight! Or I don't know what ails them at all?'

'My soul from the devil, I don't know what ails them,' said he. 'Some of the old foolishness, I suppose.'

'There isn't an old woman or a young woman in the top of the hamlet who is not gone west to the top of the shore,' said I.

'I wonder what do they want west?' said he, and a kind of wonder on him.

'Old Nell told me the fish was shoaling in the Yellow Island beach, and that the fishermen were in a way to drown each other over them, and I suppose she's right because I have the noise of the world to hear west from me for a while,' said I.

''Tis no wonder you would,' said he, 'because the evening is delightful and the appearance of fish is on the sea.'

Just then who'd come from east to us only the Yank and he hurrying. It was very hard to understand two of them there talking together and I beckoned the ass with me. When I came to the house I hadn't a Christian of the Son of Judgment to be seen over or hither. They had all gone west to see the wrangling. I threw the potato bags off the ass's back and I left him there picking for himself. But it's not picking he went but plundering. There was a next-door neighbour's bag of potatoes beside the bank because she didn't wait to put it in the shed. When she saw everyone running, she ran herself and left the bag there; and what do you say to the old white ass but that he found it out, and though he was old he was not wanting in teeth. It wasn't a long delay on him tearing the bag. As soon as he tore the bag the potatoes went with the slope. Then there was the scuffle, because there was a group of geese in the milking-field and here's for the potatoes with them in freedom. Each goose had his own knop in his beak, and as we know, that didn't put any check on the old white ass, for he was chewing at his best. Here's me to him and a stump of a stick in my hand.

'Musha, the curse of God and His church on you, you rogue!' said I. 'If it's not you that is up to your job! If Old Nell finds out that 'twas you tore the pack, the end of it will never be heard.'

I hit a flip of the stick on him and put him into the shed before he'd go eating the potatoes again and be caught at it.

When I came back, who would be standing in the doorway but Long Sean, a boy who was spending his holidays in the island.

'Sean,' said I, 'since nobody else is in charge of the house only you at the moment, do some aid to the bag of potatoes the animals have torn asunder. Look the geese themselves are having a time on them.'

'By my baptism, I won't!' said he. 'Why didn't they stay in charge of them? It's not of my care. Let them mind them. If they were fretting about them it's not there they'd leave them.'

'Musha, the bonham's baptism on you!' said I. 'Would it matter who'd do the good deed?'

'It wouldn't indeed,' said Sean, 'but we'll have subject for amusement in a while, when Nell comes home.'

My own patience broke and I put the scattering of the small birds on the geese.

'It's not looking at the sport you are, Sean,' said I, 'or where were you?'

'Town with Thomas, the poet,[1] and I don't know on earth where all the people are gone.'

'Look over west towards the top of the shore and you'll see where they are. And if you're short of Gaelic, on my soul it's there you'll get it.'

'I suppose so; but I wouldn't understand as much as a word from them. As we know, they're quicker with their tongue than the Greek himself, especially when they're excited. There's nobody I understand better than you and Thomas.'

'Hadn't you better go west to see the sport?' said I.

'Can't we see enough of them from this place?' said Sean.

'But you'd have amusement on the old women. Look, they're in a way to get at each other's windpipes.'

'It will be a furious fight amongst them!' said Sean.

'It's certain it will,' said I. 'They are talking into each other's mouths already.'

'Does this caper be going on usually, Peig?'

'I never noticed such wrangling before, Sean, and much less did I see such a sight since I came to the island. The sea is coloured black with canoes and the fish so plentiful at the surface of the water that it would put joy on anyone. Look at the driving the canoes have and the clattering they have.'

'There are more than the island's canoes there,' said Sean.

'The canoes of Dunquin and the canoes of Ventry, and if I'd say it, from Moortown, and no wonder there's wrangling,

[1] Tomás Ó Crohan, author of *The Islandman*.

and enthusiasm in the women, because the men are out in a way to drown each other. Aren't they a nice sight?' said I.

'Nice, indeed,' said Sean. 'Many a person would like to see them.'

'It's glorious weather, Sean. The air at the bottom of the sky is as yellow as gold, and the reflection of the rocks is out in the water. There's not a breath blowing, but calm and beauty, and the fish so plentiful at the surface of the water. It was true for the poet when he made the hymn long ago:

> 'Praise and gratitude to you, Holy Father,
> Who created the skies and heaven first
> And after that created the big wet sea
> And the heaps of fish in it swimming closely.'

'Oh! great and widespread are God's gifts, praise for ever to Him!' said Sean.

'Great,' said I. 'Wouldn't the sight you see before you make you understand the grace of God? But I'm afraid the fishermen will have little of it, because it's seldom they succeed in killing any fish when it's on the surface like that too early in the evening.'

'Do you say so?' said Sean.

'I don't know, by my crook,' said I, 'but it's often I saw the canoes around them like that and no fish would go in a net out of it, and the fishermen say that 'tis how the weather is too bright. But isn't it teatime for you, Sean?'

'It is,' said he, 'but I suppose there's nobody at the house yet,' and he went from me west.

About ten o'clock or so he came to us again, because it was his way to spend a while of the night with us.

'God your welcome!' said I. 'Have you any new story since?'

'I have and a bagful,' said he.

'Take the string off your mouth and let's have them,' said I.

'Tut, woman. If I took the cord off, they'd go all over the dishes on me, like the potatoes went a while ago. I'd rather be telling them to you one by one. But the first story I have to tell you is that you have a sort of second sight. You told me this evening there was danger that it was a big pregnancy coming as a dead calf, for the man of the house said when he came home that there wasn't a fish killed in the bay tonight, and wasn't it awful work and the fish so plentiful?'

'Musha, blinding and confusion on them!' said I. 'It is ever said that no work is the better for a crowd of women to be watching it. If the women stayed at home, maybe the matter wouldn't be as it is.'

'God with my soul!' said Sean, 'you know there's no harm like that in them.'

'Arrah, man, the superstitions of the world follow women pedlars. The fishermen are always fleeing from them,' said I.

'Anyway,' said Sean, 'they hadn't the fish. But the woman of our house was more concerned about the bag of potatoes that was gone to loss than all the fish from Bray Head to here. I think when she came home Aristotle himself wouldn't understand her although he was a clever man. Devil a word I understood from her, anyway. I think she's in the same driving still but she can't work off her temper on anyone, but herself.'

We had no chance of further talk that night, because a little girl came calling Sean.

'Your supper is ready!' and she turned on her heel without making delay.

'All right, all right, I'll be coming,' said Sean, and he stuck his hands in his overcoat and put the shape for the road on himself. 'Goodnight to you, Peig!' said he, and went out the door slant-shouldered.

Before that or since there didn't come such a sight of fish. A fisherman from Ventry parish who was there said that he didn't see at a race or a fair a sight that would beat what he saw that evening with the yellowing of the sun in the shore of the Yellow Island. But anything has but a while up and down in all this life. The fishing is failed for years, but as the scholar said to the pagan long ago: 'The foetus turns', and maybe the fishing will come ahead yet, with the help of God. It's one of God's gifts and He never put a bush in the opening of a haven.

CHAPTER THIRTEEN

A Milk-House in Little Island;
Nance Daly and Nora Keaveney

Many an old woman in Ireland had a nicer place and more pleasant to study than this, but I prefer this lonely place to any other place in Ireland. The golden mountains of Ireland are without mist before me. The sea is pouring itself against the rocks and running up in dark ravines and caves where the seals live. We are not disturbed by the uproar and noise of the city. There is a fine hedge around us and we are inside the Summerhouse of Peace. There is no picture-house only these lovely things God created, praise for ever to Him! Every time I get the chance I give a run to get a view of these things which are most pleasant to my heart. Little Island is before me and white sheep in their fleeces grazing there where my mother remembered, when she was young, milk to be, and butter being made in plenty.

'Tis well I remember, and I looking from me on this island, listening to my father and I a little girl talking about the people who were living in Little Island at that time, and in many other places. 'Tis little I thought then that I'd be living so near to that island. But since I'm sitting here, looking over at it, see how the thoughts run far back into the years that are gone by me—to the little solitary house at the foot of the hills again. It's a little thatched house. It's where I was born and reared. There's an old ruin a bit over from it, where Maurice Scanlan was, where I spent the days of my childhood. I see, I think, Maurice himself standing in the doorway, and he giving sweets to us, after his coming from Dingle. I see, I think, my mother sitting in the corner and Nell Malone and Old Mary O'Connor, and they talking about the things they remembered in their early youth. See Kate, my brother's wife, busy about the house and myself in the corner, rocking the cradle, heeding and giving ear to my mother telling this story to the others:

'Long years after the bad times and the famine,' said she, 'much of the land of Ireland was derelict. The poor people who used to inhabit it were gone the way of truth with the hunger and want. Those of them who managed to live, and had a piece of land, had big rent to pay and the hardship of life working violently on them, and when they couldn't pay the rent they got nothing but the side of the road distressfully and their house burnt.

'As I said before, the land was derelict and there was no gain from it for the landlord. The plan he made was to put milk-houses, or *dairies* as they were called, here and there, put servants in charge of them, and put milch-cows on the land. I remember well two of them to be in Dunquin, one of them west there at the Shed and another down at the Milk Crossroads. He put another on Little Island, with a married couple minding it, a man named Richard O'Carroll and Kate Daly, or Kate from Little Island, as she was called. Kate was clever and she had good knowledge of butter and milk. She had two sisters, Brigid and Nance. It's Brigid was at the Milk Crossroads and Nance was at the Shed. There was no limit with them for minding butter and milk. None of them was married but Kate, and she had no offspring. She and her husband were living snugly with no want from the Lord. A big boat was serving them frequently. They had a nice comfortable house in Little Island, and if they hadn't a nice airly little island, it's not a day yet. There was nothing Kate lacked more than water,

because there was no spring-water well in Little Island, and
'tis how Richard O'Carroll had to bring little barrels of
water from the Heel of the Island. Often it wasn't calm,
and the poor man would risk drowning; but long as he was
succeeding, providence got a chance on him and he was
drowned, may they be safe where it is told! That gave its
name to the Heel since—O'Carroll's Heel it's called.

'That put an end to butter and milk and living in Little
Island. Poor Kate had to leave the place and face out
somewhere else to earn her living.

'As I said before, her sister, Nance, was a milk-woman
at the Shed. She was a lovely young woman, and it was no
wonder the young men were looking after her. Small
interest Nance had in any of them but one man, that is,
Young Sean O'Flaherty. He was her total share of the men
of the world and she wouldn't allow any other girls to wink
at him. But Young Sean wasn't so senseless after her. Over
there he was living where Owen Brown's house is today.
There was nobody in the house but himself and his sister,
Kate. Their parents were on the way of truth for years
before that and as we know they had to fend for themselves.
So, when Kate got the chance she married a man from
Coom named Sean Brosnahan. That left Young Sean alone
and he had to marry to have a housewife. Nance thought,
no wonder, that she'd be that woman—there was nothing
to upset her with him. She had an overwhelming love for
him and she thought that he had the same for her, but he
hadn't. Love is a thing that torment and torture follows
and often it's not lasting, and it's a small thing that upsets it.
That's how it happened to Nance Daly.

'Shrovetide came and there was a wedding on in Flagstone Glen and there were many girls from the south parish
at the wedding, and they neatly dressed in the fashion of
that time. Whoever was at that wedding, Young Sean

O'Flaherty was there and many a young girl was looking under her eyelashes and making honey in her heart of his good looks, because he was a proportionately-made young man, brown curly hair on him, a flush in his cheeks, and two grey eyes in his head that would make any dear girl like him.

'There was a party of the girls sitting on a seat in a lonely corner of the house, and the devil to Sean but he noticed them and went where they were. After a little talk he told one of them to sing a song, but she said she couldn't, that she never sang any song. He continued urging from one to the other until he went to the fifth girl. She took courage and she said "I'll sing a song for you, good man!" She caught him by the hand and she started on this song:

> My great loss and my grief
> And my visit this way,
> My parents will be grieved
> Asking about me of everyone.
> I gave you great love
> Over the boys of Ireland,
> Until I'm stretched in the grave
> I will not forsake your merriment.
>
> Had I a box full of gold
> And a chest full of silver,
> I would give it to Sean
> He's the commanding hearty.
> Isn't it happy for the woman
> Who will get you tied from the priest!
> But my want through my heart
> Is that I am for ever parted from you!

' "Forever! Forever!" said he, "What is your name, young woman? Your name, please? Tell it to me!" and he spoke very quietly, because Nance was sitting near the table and her eyes sharp peeping on him.

' "Nora Keaveney," said she, "and it's in Ventry parish my parents live."

' "You are my choice above any girl I have seen yet, and if you gave me your hand I'd have no other wife but you," said he, and he moved up to her, saying those words.

' "Have my promise and my word, if my parents agree to it."

' "All right," said Sean, and his heart was as light as a blackbird, because he had given the love of his breast to Nora at that moment. It was no wonder he had, because she was a pretty, gentle girl, with skin as white as the swan, her cheeks as red as the rose, and curly black hair on her. She was proportionately made and it would be hard to find fault with her.

'Next day Sean and a lad with him went off, and nobody knew where he was until he came back to Vicarstown with Nora Keaveney married. Then the row was on. When Nance Daly heard that her dear love was married to another woman, she nearly lost her mind. She used to be watching Nora, day and night like a cat would be watching a mouse. It was dangerous for Nora to put her head out the door, because Nance was always watching her. Poor Nora had no idea why Nance should be that way. If she had known the great love Nance had for Young Sean she wouldn't have been so haughty as she was, coming, but nobody gave her that information.

'One day at the beginning of spring, Sean was working in the field, and when Nora had the potatoes for the dinner drained, she went out on the garden fence and called her husband aloud, but she didn't manage to make the second call when Nance had a shower of stones all around her. Barely she got her soul inside with her, because when she was standing inside on the floor Nance aimed at her with a rough stone that knocked the side out of the potato-pot beside her. The poor girl was frightened. When Sean came home he knew that Nora was not easy in her mind.

' "What's wrong with you?" said he.

' "I'm frightened alive by a woman without sense that's around there," said Nora. "I don't know who she is or what she has against me, but she's after me every day since I reached this house. And look, she has broken the potato-pot today, but I don't care in the devil, so long as it's not my head she has broken. Do you know why she's like that?"

' "It's all the same to you about her—don't pretend that you hear her, but when dinner is ready put a white rag on the gable, and I'll come home."

'Yes, the year was slipping by and if Nance was tormented, she had a kind of surrender to her enemy, Nora, because she was going to have a young child for Christmas.

'A daughter was born to Nora, and because of milk being scarce 'tis how she was buying milk in the house of White Dermot who was living down at the bridge. One morning, after the morning meal, Nora told her husband to stay and mind the baby while she'd be fetching the milk. She took a jug with her and went down the road. But Nance was not snoozing, for she saw Nora going down the road. She decided it was a good time to catch up even with her. The envy and the old love were fighting each other in her heart still, and she made out she could get some vengeance on Nora because she was the top and bottom of her heart's torment. She had a bitter hatred for her and it would be great ease of mind for her if she could get revenge on her this way or that way. On that, she followed Nora to White Dermot's house. Poor Nora was only in across the threshold when Nance was in on her heels. She had the look of anger. She was a hard strong woman and it was no wonder Nora would be afraid of her. She spoke to the woman of the house.

' "Have you milk for me today, Molly?" said she.

' "Indeed I haven't, O daughter," said Molly. "I have the last drop sent in the vessel to this good woman here."

'Nance didn't need but "I want a reason" and her eyes lit with the flame of anger, and she said with strong, fearless voice:

' "She won't have my milk!" said she. "It's enough for her to have my dear love and the man who took my sense from me—but he won't have much good in her after me," and she shaped to fight.

'When Nora saw her with the crossing shape on her, she decided she had better stand her ground and defend herself as best in Ireland she could do. Before Nance had a chance to say "God with my soul", Nora had jumped out of herself like a wildcat, gripping her by the hair of her head. With the first twist she gave her she knocked Nance down on the floor. "Yes, girl," said she, "that's the recommendation of two people from the Big Cliff for you—whichever of us is strongest be uppermost—and as I am uppermost I'll put the mark of my limbs to be seen by everybody on you. And if you loved Young Sean O'Flaherty, he had no love for you, and I have himself and his love and his baby, and you whistle away for yourself!"

'Such wrangling and biting Moll never saw before. The flame was in her eyes looking at them. But much as Nance Daly was inclined for fight, she was as gentle as a sheep's lamb when Nora parted with her. She scraped and scratched and cut her so that there was a red brand on Nance.

' "Go now," said Nora, "and don't tell where you were, and don't look over your shoulder at me as long as you live. The lovely looks you had coming, it's different appearance you have now! But when you're healed you can give your love to somebody other than Sean O'Flaherty."

'She took the milk-jug that was on the table and little grass grew under her feet until she reached home. She suspected that Nance would follow her and split her with stones, but she didn't. She was sour enough with herself and ashamed of the mistake she had made. From that day until she left the Shed she didn't look over her shoulder at Nora Keaveney.'

The long years are gone in a gallop, and these who are in the life of my story gone too, as the mist goes with the wind. I can see today only the place where they used to live, but they draw me back on the lonely road of thoughts, and 'tis nice how Youth pays me a small visit, when I'm at tight grips with the years. I am young again, I think. There is courage and merriment in my heart. I feel the mind as strong and courageous as ever it was. But when the fine pleasant thoughts go, rust and sourness and weakness of the brain comes on me and I feel some heavy weight coming down on my heart.

Maybe the reader has youth in power. If so, he feels the heart light and secure, the laugh clean, the jump musical, the jollity and merriment, the brightness and freshness and fragrance everywhere on his way. I remember having all those little jewels myself, but see how the ugly thief age came and stole them from me! Great as the guarding is, he sneaks upon us. Nobody feels him coming.

CHAPTER FOURTEEN

The Quarrel about Hens in Dunquin

'Where were you, Michael?' said I.

'I was over there east at the gable of Dermot's house listening to Old Mary and Nell. Such clamour they had about hens I never heard.'

'Isn't it great that there'd have to be always an argument between them?' said I.

'Mary suspects that her hen is laying in Nell's place, and Nell is denying in the matter, and that's the reason of the argument,' said Michael.

'Musha, it's a queer thing that the women never agreed with each other,' said I. 'Wherever they'll be they'll have some gib-gab going on. But look, that reminds me of the quarrel two women had in our hamlet when I was a little one growing up. It was a hen was the cause of that quarrelling too, and such a reviling and disputing of words they had! It wasn't one day that was going on but throughout the year.

'These two women I say were living in the two houses nearest to each other and they were always in dispute with each other, because one was no more fluent with the tongue than the other. I think the vein of poetry was in each of them by birth and it's often we'd be listening to them when there would be any argument between them.

'I remember an evening when I was in Little Brigid's house, myself and Kate Jim and Nell Brigid, and we learning our lessons for tomorrow. Brigid herself was sitting on a seat and a fine red fire before us. There were two girls spinning, girls related to Brigid. They had two spinning

wheels and they were spinning perfectly. Tim Sean, the man of
the house, was sitting on a chair making a basket of green
briars and now and again you'd hear him put a grunt from
him when the thorns would prick him. Everyone was quiet
only Mary, one of the girls who were spinning. She was
singing, and she was a fine singer. But it wasn't long until
the song stopped because Kate James, the next-door neighbour, came in. She saluted, but the answer she got from
Little Brigid was not too kind.

' "What's wrong with you now, Brigid?" said Kate, "or
what anger is this? You have something going on again—
or what reached your ears that put the surge of anger
on you?"

' "Musha, I'm hearing a lot this weather," said Brigid.

' "Maybe it's the lie you hear," said Kate.

'They had from the small word to the big word in that
way, until Brigid said in a loud voice:

' "Do you know who you're talking to? To a woman who
came from a hamlet which cannot be accused of anything
from any side of the sides. Here they are for you, girl!"
said she, and she stretched herself. "The clean people of
Brown Hill, the spotless Mannion people, Moriartys of
goodwill and the White Connells—and isn't it hard to
revile them?"

' "I don't mind about the relations," said Kate, "but
tell me what put the anger on you."

' "The woman of the house up here who has me wronged
about my hen, and I'm full sure it's my own hen."

' "Maybe it is and maybe it isn't," said Kate. "There
could be a mistake in the matter. It's often I saw people
full sure about certain things and be very much mistaken
about them, and maybe it's the same way with you."

' "Oh! yes, just," said Brigid. "You, too, are against me.
Ye are a ship of the same timber. Have the door for yourself!

Leave my house!" and she lit with anger. Kate got up quickly and when she was going out the door she spoke aloud:

' "To the devil I commit you and your hippish hut!" said she.

'Only for how quickly she was clear of the doorway she'd have a lump on her head from the sod of hard peat turf, from Brigid, because she took noise out of the door with the sod.

'The cause of the talk and all the anger was a hen that was in dispute between Little Brigid and White Mary. Maureen, White Mary's daughter, got a hen as a present from her aunt when Maureen was on a visit to her a while before that. When the hen was in a strange place the little creature used to be going alone because of the other hens pecking her. But at last she settled down with Brigid's hens and then Brigid wanted to say it was her own and she wouldn't let little Maureen or her mother go near it. I needn't say but they had great talk and disputing and there was nothing in the people's mouths but themselves—Brigid always saying that the hen belonged to her own sister who had gone to America a while before that, and White Mary arguing it was not so, that it was her own daughter got it from her aunt. The shape or skin of the hen wasn't worth the amount of talk was made of it.

'At last the aunt, Nora O'Shea, heard of the quarrel of the hen and another thing she heard that Brigid said if Nora recognized the hen, she would settle. Therefore Nora decided to pay them the visit on the coming Sunday, and after Mass that day she went in to Brigid.

' "Musha, a hundred welcomes before you, Nora!" said Brigid.

' "May ye live strong and well!" said Nora.

' "I suppose it's the hen-quarrel that brought you to us?" said Brigid.

' "It is indeed," said Nora. "It's a great shame for next-door neighbours to be in disagreement with each other over a paltry little thing that's not worth mentioning."

' "Musha, you're right," said Brigid, "but when you'd be sure you owned it, it would be hard for you to part with it. But if you make out it's yours the matter will be a calm peace with us."

' "If I saw her I should recognize her," said Nora.

'Then Brigid stood up and put some food on a dish in the middle of the house and she called the hens. Soon there were over forty hens around the dish and a stranger of a big red cockerel with three inches of a big double comb on him, and he wouldn't prove a good share to anyone who would interfere with the hens.

' "God with my soul! You have a flock of them!" said Nora.

' "I have," said Brigid, "most of them stayed with me after my sister who went to America lately."

'Nora was looking closely at them, and at last she stood up, and down with her to where they were eating. She caught the hen of the dissent and picked it up.

' "That's the hen I gave to Maureen," said she. "Keep her or give her from you!"

'Before the word was out of her mouth the cockerel had jumped out of himself and he was entangled in her legs and had a painful peck given to her in the back of her hand. She was anxious letting the hen go, because her legs were well scratched.

' "Musha, it's an old proverb," said she, "and it's true, that the peacemaker doesn't go free!" and she took herself out the door.

' 'Twas after her going home they had all the arguing because they started to make verses of poetry for each other. A short while after that there wasn't in the mouths of the children of the hamlet but the apt talk that two women gave to each other.'

'Have you the verses, Peig?' said Michael, 'I would like to hear some of "The Quarrel of the Hens in Dunquin".'

'Here it is for you, then,' said I and I started to sing these verses:

BRIGID:
Mary Joan is on the upper side of the hill from me
Cursing me every day about my hen;
But I ask my Master and bright Mary, his Mother,
That they find shame as they gave to me.

WHITE MARY:
No benefit to the prattler the quiet proud girl
To be sitting here beside her on the upper side of the hill;
Of the breed of the men who were tall and bright,
And isn't it hard for ever to put her from her surname.

BRIGID:
It's not your hen at all but my sister's hen,
Which she left to me when she went over the sea.
Mary Joan is saying it's hers
And may little Mary not benefit, doing without it.

WHITE MARY:
She is the gabber of an arrogant yellow hag
Who has a lot of it her mind and will for ever,
Who stole my child's hen which came from over the hillock
And may she never much increase her purse.

BRIGID:
I hope the Virgin will keep me like unto her
However long my life be now in the crowd;
But I saw her awhile and she had nothing
And wouldn't all her life only for women's heritage.

'They continued that way but it was very soon they had another care on them, because when they were strongest was when they were nearest to losing their feathers. Like a hundred others, their heads were laid low by a sick bout that finished all the arguing; and I think that's the same way with these two women of ours, too.'

'I don't know in the world, Peig, but they're going in each other's combs about the hens on the east side of the hamlet. I'm thinking for a long time that the black pig[1] is living between the two glens.'

'May God not allow that, Michael!' said I.

'Oh! God allows it, little woman,' said Michael, and he put fire to his pipe and went strolling for himself the road west to the beach.

[1] A harbinger of woe, in folk-belief.

CHAPTER FIFTEEN

'Martin Monday' a Gaelic Speaker from Mexico

My love God, it puts great joy on my old heart to hear the Gaelic language being spoken by the grandees and nobles of the country! When I was a little girl earning the bread in Dingle, it's little I thought that the way of today would be heard. But the longer a person lives the more he'll have to tell. The proverb says that all good comes given time, and grace with patience. At that time we'd be ashamed and head-bent for not having little or more English. Small respect anyone had for us—'The Asses of the Island', the Dingle people used to call us. I remember well 'twas often a big man used to come in to us, with sarcasm in his stranger mouth and breathing on his speech. You'd hear the ugly echoes he'd take out of the rafters of the house, with 'Good morning, sir', or 'Good morning, madam', and you'd hear the answer 'How are you getting along, sir?' It would make me sick to be listening to them. But it is ever said 'If it's a wrong, it will return', and the mocking they'd make about us at that time, we are able to give to them today as lavishly as they gave it to us, because it's few people are brought to this island who are not able to speak to us in our own language.

One of these I made great wonder of was Martin Dillon, or 'Martin Monday', as the island people christened him. A stranger from Mexico, who came lately to us, a gentle youth and a clever scholar. It's often he'd be on a visit to us and he was the accurate historian—his master I never met yet. I was astonished how he had managed to have the Gaelic so fluently, and I questioned him about it.

'Don't be surprised,' said he, 'at the Gaelic being so fluent with me, because my mother had it and she never hid it from me.'

'But how did it happen that that noble gem stayed with your mother?' said I.

'It stayed,' said he; 'she kept it alive in fond memory of the place she was born, in Iveragh, and she had limitless love for that place. "My lovely sun-home", she used always call it, for she used to be telling us stories about that place when we were children growing up. I remember well the evening she was telling us about the hardship she had from her youth, and that that was why she had no love for the stranger language. Although we were living in Mexico, far from the company of Gaels or Gaelic-speakers, Gaelic was the fireside language my father and mother used to speak to us. Although English was being used in Mexico, Spanish was the common language there. My mother had little knowledge of Spanish so Gaelic was the language she preferred to speak to us.

'She was only nine years of age,' said he, 'when the bailiffs came to the door to them and threw them out on the road and set fire to the little house they had. 'Tis how they were mocking at the mother when she was beating her hands and crying bitterly. What would she do with her young family, or where would she go with them for the night? But little heed had they for the beating of hands.

'The neighbours made up some little shelter for them for the night, but it was the cold place. The woman and the four children had to live there, but the mother lived only twelve days. She died of grief and heartbreak, and that left my mother with a burden because she had to fend for her brothers who were young and weak. But God helps weakness and as she was growing older she was managing better to aid them and keep them at school. Her father had to be working for the neighbours, because he had neither house nor land then. But they were doing well, for when my mother was eighteen years of age her aunt in California sent her her fare. She managed to get to her and she wasn't long with her aunt when she got work in a good house. As soon as she had any small sum of money earned, she was thinking more about her father and her brothers than about herself. When her oldest brother was twenty years of age, she sent him his fare, and across the sea with him. He got good work, too, and often the two of them were on a visit to their aunt's house, and 'twas she was proud of my mother. It was no wonder, because she was a sensible, modest girl who could easily accept good advice from her aunt.

' 'One evening, walking alone, she saw a lovely young lad before her in the street. A kind of worry came on her because she perceived that she should recognize him. As soon as he stood in front of her she saluted him with God and Mary and he saluted her, mannerly and softly, with God and Mary and Patrick.

' "Thanks to God," said she, "for a man to meet me in a foreign street who can answer me in my own language! Where are you from, good man?"

' "I am a Kerryman and in Kenmare I lived."

' "What family are you from?" said she.

' "Of the Dillon people—James Dillon are my name and surname," said he.

' "And it's from Glenbeigh I am," said she. "Isn't it lucky how we met each other! I'll have a companion now."

'They walked together until they went to her aunt's house, and it's on her the great surprise was when she saw the stranger.

' "Where did you meet this young man?" said she, "or who is he?"

' "He is a friend of ours, Aunt," said she, "and a next-door neighbour; and it's near a miracle that we should meet so far from home. James Dillon are his name and surname and it's from Kenmare he came."

' "Wherever he's from he has the appearance of a good man," said the aunt, "and I have a hundred welcomes before you."

'That was the first evening they became acquainted, but it wasn't the last evening with them, for every time he got the chance he'd come on a visit to them. It was very soon both their minds were in one mind and they at their best to save a little before settling down. He was earning a good big pay, because 'tis how he was working on a big ship that was going from California to Mexico and every run he'd do he'd be watching closely to see if he'd find any nice place to settle in. At last he decided on a place that was, he thought, satisfactory. On a visit he paid to my mother he disclosed his secret and told her that he had a place decided in Mexico if she would like it and if she would wish to pay a visit there to see it in a couple of days.

' "I'll go anywhere with you," said she, "but I'll have to place it in my aunt's permission first, for I have no other mother but herself."

'In a couple of days after that she was aboard a ship that was sailing to Mexico, but she had only a short visit there.

'Two months after that my mother and father were married in California. They gathered their things and bade farewell to the aunt and went to Mexico to dwell, where I was born and reared. I have three brothers and a sister and all of them can speak Gaelic as well as I. That's my story for you, woman of the house.'

'Great God, Martin,' said I, 'it's no wonder that you are proud of your mother, and to say that she kept the Gaelic alive and bestowed it on you as a gem.'

'I would never be satisfied without seeing the place where my mother was born. That's why I came all the way. It won't be long more until my visit is finished, and indeed I'll be lonely.'

'Musha, may God bring you safe, Martin!' said I, 'and bring my good wishes to your mother when you are going.'

CHAPTER SIXTEEN

The News of the 1916 Revolution: the Black-and-Tans' Visit

Long years after my coming to the island there was clamour and confusion, that there was a destroying battle between Irish and Strangers in Dublin. At first you wouldn't believe a word of it. A big story, a wonderful story it was. The postman brought us the story, may God grant his soul eternal rest! He said that Dublin City was one huge fire and the big guns of the Stranger battering it and the fragrant blood of the Irish being spilled.

'The Irish are awake again,' said he, 'and the people are stirred as I never saw them; and it's danger in my mind that life won't be too peaceful with Yellow John!'[1]

'You saying it and God to answer you!" said Big Owen O'Sullivan who was putting tobacco in his pipe. 'Material for intelligence for ye, men, that it wasn't without authority the Volunteers were drilling. The day came at last when they were able to strike a blow on their enemy.'

'On my soul, Owen,' said Old Michael, greatly stirred, 'but it will be paid for dearly, because great as our hate for England is, great and wonderful is the strength she has. We heard that the sun never set on her lands.'

'Yellow John will want them all, Old Michael, before he is finished with the People of Ireland, if today's story is true.'

'I suppose, musha, that in Irish talk there was never but cliff grass compared with this heavy blow that has

[1] A name for John Bull.

been struck in the Royal City of Ireland, if it's true.'

'If it's true,' said the King,[2] with sarcasm in his voice. 'As sure as there's grey whiskers on your jawbone the heaviest beating that was ever beaten in Ireland is going on there. And worse than that there's a warship firing in on the city. They say total destruction is done already there. I heard that the girls of the city were fighting shoulder to shoulder with the lads, my music they!'

' 'Twas of their ancestors' kind to have the noble royal drop in them,' said Big John Carney, 'but my regret and worry, the enemy is too strong, I fear, and they will be vanquished early! Did you hear was there any stirring being done by the other people of Ireland?'

'I did. They are already preparing themselves for the battle, but 'tis said that it's not to Dublin they are inclined to go but that 'tis how they'll be engaging the enemy in battle here and there. But many of the Volunteers are facing for Dublin. It seems they would rather fall in the battle than let the enemy go victorious.'

'May God join strength with the lads!' said Big Owen. 'The King's barracks will be knocked down again and Yeomen being hunted by us.'

'By my palms but the day is after coming at last,' said Old Michael, 'but this won't do. Words don't fatten the brothers!' and he threw his bag over his back.

It wasn't long after that until the battle was on all over Ireland. There wasn't to be heard from morning till night but War, War, War—in the air over us and all around us. The man who would be herding his stock at the top of the hill, when he'd come home, the first question he'd ask was, 'Is there any story from the War today?' or 'Which side is giving in?' He'd have terror in him; you'd think it was a spirit or some pooka he saw on the mountain, but it wasn't;

[2] The King was the postman.

'tis how he'd be upset in his mind. There was a man in this hamlet at that time and wherever he'd go there'd be the smell of powder. In the wind that was blowing from west over the top of Maam, he was being suffocated by the ugly smell of powder. But the little boys were not very grateful to him, for often he sent them running for their lives up the side of the hill, persuading them the sky was on fire in the west and that the strong smell of powder was being blown before the wind, and sparks of fire. The poor boys were so disturbed then that they'd believe him. When they'd get to the top of the hill they couldn't see anything but the white slender legs of the north wind. If they had hold of him then they'd take the grey whisker off his jawbone, but he'd be fast asleep, without any heed for them.

I remember a morning I was up very early because I had a good lot of work to do. When I put my head to the door, it would be a good person the delight of that hour wouldn't lift the mist from his heart. The sea was smooth and slippery, and the dew heavy on the grass and the sun beating over the back of Eagle Mountain as red as a piece of old gold. If I had pen and ink then wouldn't I describe well the delight of that morning. Many a nice colour I had to be seen with the rising of the sun—the gulls on the beach, the lark above me singing his pure gentle song and more, if I mentioned them. But it was soon those nice things were put astray on me, because I saw a man running east the road. He startled me, because it's seldom you'd see a man running like that, and soon there was another man galloping after him. 'Yes,' said I to myself, 'something has happened.' I moved out and I was peeping, but if so, I had nothing to see. But soon I got the release from my task because a little boy came across.

'Musha, Johnny, my treasure,' said I, 'what's going on

down at the harbour that has all the people gathered there so early in the morning?'

'There are,' said he, 'two lads from Dingle who came fleeing for their lives this morning. English they were speaking and I didn't pick with my ears only this much —' and he stopped.

'And what is it?' said I and eagerness on me to hear the story.

'Musha, I don't know did my ears take it with them correctly.'

'Speak, man, speak! Let it to me!' said I.

' "ALL JOHN STREET IS BURNED!" ' said he.

'And who burned it?' said I.

'Don't ask me,' said he, 'I don't understand any English,' and he went from me airily for himself.

'It's a pity everyone isn't as innocent as you, boy,' said I. 'But welcome the grace of God! The blood is being spilled at our door at last. I suppose 'tis how the Irish made an attack on them in Dingle. If so, I suppose people fell on both sides.'

Before I had time to put more questions to myself, who would come in but Old Nell, my next-door neighbour.

'Musha, Peig, my heart,' said she, 'how can you be so worldly and the end of the world upon us?'

'Musha, welcome to it!' said I, 'but this war won't end the world, or the war that will come after it. It's not wars, but God Himself, praise for ever to Him! will end it. And, poor woman, if it's for you or me to fall in this war, don't you think that better people than us will fall in it?'

'That's true, Peig, but as we know, that wouldn't take the fear off me, to know that a better person than I would fall in the fray. Didn't you hear that the battle was going on in Dingle?'

'If I did, I have no correct authority for it.'

'But indeed, my pet, it's true. There are two lads from Dingle in the hamlet since the end of the night. There was a battle on and the commander of the Stranger army was killed, and more of his men.'

'Were any of the Volunteers laid low?' said I.

'I didn't hear that there were,' said she, 'but Dingle is to be set on fire because madness and anger grip the Strangers and I suppose wholesale plundering is afoot there by now.'

'It's not, Nell,' said I. 'Have sense. A different story will be heard tomorrow.'

'May God let good stories of the best to us!' said Nell. 'I am afraid because the enemy is too clever, too treacherous always.'

'Hush your mouth, woman! God is stronger than hope! Didn't you ever hear "At the height of the storm help is nearest?" Aren't we far west from them and we should have no fear. It's not worth their while coming to this sea island.'

'On my own palms, musha,' said Nell, 'but I heard people saying that they were going to pay it a visit, far west as it is. They suspect there's an army hidden here and you wouldn't know but it would be in the middle of the night they'd knock on your door. They are clean out of their minds because of how true the Irish are to each other. They thought, the fools, that they had only to come, because they thought they hadn't before them in this little country but people of no heed. But it's clear to them today that it's soul-gambling seriously for them to meet the lads. There's wonder and amazement on them where are the arms coming from to them. I wouldn't be a bit surprised if they hopped in to us. This island of ours is lonely and, in their mind, useful for hiding arms, and they have an enormous suspicion of us.'

'Musha, if they come itself,' said I, 'they won't have but "An idle journey and a dead sheep", as the woman said long ago.'

But Nell was right, because a couple of days after that there was no canoe in Dunquin but was in to us full of people. The Stranger soldiers it was. They made the Dunquin people take them to the island. They dug their heels in at first that they wouldn't come with them, but the soldiers threatened arms on them and the poor people had to give in, though against their will.

When they came in then there was the wrangling because they were sure the island was blown up in the sky and everything in it burnt, both houses and people. The end of the world was there that day, we thought. As we know, we never saw the war forces, and signs on it—you wouldn't lay an eye on anyone who had his own natural colour.

I was sitting by the fire, drinking a cup of tea, as usual, when Eileen my daughter ran in the door and terror in her.

'Oh! God·with us, Mammy, all the soldiers and guns that are about the hamlet—and what are you doing?'

'I am eating, my girl,' said I. 'If it's death itself for me it's a great thing to be strong for the long road.'

'I suppose,' said she, 'there will be no house or person on the island but will be burned to the ground.'

'Don't mind that, my pet,' said I. 'We'll all be together in the name of God.'

The word wasn't out of my mouth when Patrick, my husband, the blessing of God with his soul, came in, and mad rushing on him.

'For God's sake,' said he, 'have you no anxiety only eating and drinking, and your eating and drinking to be ended immediately. Hurry and take down those pictures on the wall!'[3]

[3] Pictures of Thomas Ashe and the 1916 leaders.

'Musha, defeat and wounding on those who felled them!'
said I. 'They felled them without mercy and they alive,
and it seems I have to hide the pictures from them now,
and they dead! But may I be dead and as dead as a stone
if I'll take them down in fear of any Stranger wretch! and
another thing, that big picture is so secure that Oscar[4]
couldn't pull it down, the strongest day he ever was.'

'Take it down!' said he, angry.

'I couldn't, I say. It will have to be left where it is, and
if it's the cause of our death, it's welcome. They fought and
fell for our sake, and as for Thomas Ashe's picture,' said I,
'I can't hide it from anyone.'

Before I could say 'God with my soul' the house filled in
with them. Such a sight I never saw. It's a good man they
wouldn't make tremble, hands and feet, and especially
people like us who never had any experience of military.
But I had nothing to do but take it easy. Indeed anyone
who would be there that day would laugh because we had
no understanding each other only deaf and dumb talk, and
it's very little of that was going on. It was God's will that
they went their way without doing harm or damage and
many an old woman had it in her heart and on the tip
of her tongue that they mightn't outlast the year.

There was a big long week before we came to ourselves
again.

Old Nell met me a couple of days after that.

'Arrah Blessed Mary, Peig, wasn't it a wonderful day!'
said she. 'I never made an appointment with my soul.
Great is the pity of a hamlet that they go to! and my pity
with God the people they'd work the arms on! Weren't
they the mob! I thought I was in the heart of the battle
when they gathered around me. I was a long time hearing
about war, but I've seen it now, and I'm not the better for

[4] A mythological hero.

it until the last day of my life. Musha, isn't the fine strong courage God gave to our lads that they stand without fear on the plains against those! O Mary, wasn't their skin black! You'd think it was down in the bowels of a ship they had spent their lives.'

'Whatever fear you had of them, on my soul you didn't forget to notice them well!'

'Arrah, this and that on me but it wasn't so much for liking them I was peeping at them but for dint of physical fear of them. I'd think, when one of them would move, that it was with intent to kill me. I'd think all the time the metal pistol would be stuck in my heart. Were you afraid, Peig?'

'I suppose, musha, I wasn't, Nell,' said I. 'What good was it for me to be afraid? Fear wouldn't save a person from death, as we know.'

'You are right, Peig, but believe me there were few people who weren't afraid.'

Soon after that, peace came and the terror that was on people went.

CHAPTER SEVENTEEN

I am Seeking the Widows' Pension; I am in a Motor-Car

Everyone's story is his own story and Martin's story is the money! I was often listening to a rumour that was going from mouth to mouth, that there was a pension for widows. I often asked people about it but they had no information to give me. My heart was gripped but when would I hear anything worthwhile. But long as day is, night comes and news of the pensions came, too. That's when the old widows had the confusion and believe me about it, there were no cramps on them. As for myself, I was excited, no wonder. But it's very hard for the old women of the Island to go to Dunquin because of not having the dry road and it's not always the sea is calm.

Myself and Mary John Michael decided to go to Bally-ferriter to get our ages and our marriage ages as soon as we'd get a calm day. On the Tuesday morning I just had the morning meal on the table when a messenger came from Mary. There came such worldly fussing on me that I didn't wait to eat a bite only to swallow my cup of tea as a drink. I threw off the old clothes and put on clean whole ones; and to tell the truth, they weren't half tightened on to me, because going down the path I was tightening them. But good as was the hurry I made the canoe was afloat before me and Mary settled in it.

'God with my soul,' said she, 'aren't you a long time! Or what delayed you?'

'Ah, let me be, woman, I didn't eat a bite with power of

anxiety! Don't you see my boots and I haven't fastened them yet. But I can do them here. I have the nice chance at them now. Here, let's move, in God's name.'

Because of the weather being so fine, we were not long going to Dunquin. As soon as I stood on the quay I looked up at the cliff. I thought it had the height of a mountain. I drew a sigh from my heart:

'O God of Power, Mary, is it reluctant I am to tackle the way up, or where did my strength and agility go? And worse than that, I've lost my breath, and I'll never manage to get to the top of the cliff.'

'Is it joking you are?' said Mary, 'anyone who would look at you and the flush that's in your cheek he'd swear there wasn't a thing in the world wrong with you.'

'Don't take the book by the cover, Mary,' said I, 'because I'm well used to it, the slippery side of me is turned outwards and the crooked side in.'

'Is it to talk we came here?' said Mary. 'When will we be moving?'

'Here it's with you!' said I, and we moved on. You'd think Mary was a hare, making her way up and I crawling after her and indeed I wouldn't carry a spoonful of wine after coming to Cliff Top. I had to sit and rest.

'We can never walk to Ballyferriter, Mary, if we don't get any jaunt,' said I. 'But see, there's a motor-car coming from the west. Maybe he'll go north.'

'There is, indeed,' said Mary, but before the word was out of her mouth the motor-car had stopped at the top of the cliff, a little way from us. I stood up to go and talk to the driver, but with that there was another motor-car coming up from the Field of the Wrinkle, putting road-dust in the sky. I raised my hand because I had a sort of acquaintance with the driver. He stopped the motor-car, and beckoned to us to come, and as we know it's on us the joy was that he came to us so opportunely. While you'd be clapping your two hands together he had swept us on the road north. When I got the ease I had plenty of talk with the driver.

'Yes,' said I to him, 'what we hadn't in the beginning of our lives we have it at the end of our lives. Isn't it little we thought we'd ever be going like this in a motor-car! But what would I be talking for? Isn't there many a change in the world in the forty-two years since last I went this road? At that time I hadn't to be seen but little thatched houses. But look, today, there are fine new houses, good enough for the palace of the King long ago. The fields themselves that were full of boulders and stones, they are smooth level ground today with fine fences.'

'They are, indeed,' said the driver. 'Do you see that white house in front of us on the hill?'

'I do,' said I. 'Isn't it the fine, airy place it is! Who are they who live in that fine house?'

'That's a Summer house for Nuns, O daughter!'

'Musha, glory to God on high in Heaven!' said I. 'That itself is a twist in life! A Nun's house where I remembered a miserable little thatched hut to be, and nobody living in it but an old Protestant woman called Lizzie Cox. I think she was the last of that family to live in the place. She had a small pension from the Stranger people and she kept a good grip on it until death choked her. But look who's living in it today but the godly Christian women—isn't it a lovely life we have now compared with that time?'

The driver stopped the car suddenly.

'Here, out with ye now!' said he, and he opened the door.

'Will you come out?' said I.

'I will, without doubt,' said he.

'What will you be charging us?' said I.

'I'll take nothing from ye this time, because I was coming here, too.'

'Musha, good never went wrong on anyone,' said I, 'but all the same, have a drink.'

'I'll drink a little drop, but I don't usually drink much.'

'Yes, this much won't kill you, with God's help!' said I. and we went into Mr. Long's house. I called a drink then for him. When he had drunk it he bade us farewell and went away, because his business was elsewhere and he had to be moving.

'I suppose it's this pension that's going on that brought ye?' said Mrs. Long, who was standing in the shop.

'It is, musha,' said Mary, 'and I suppose it's the idle journey for us.'

'Oh! it's not indeed. Isn't it as right for ye to have it as anyone? But I think you'll be delayed, because the priest is in Dingle, and it will be two o'clock before he comes.'

'Oh! God with my soul!' said Mary, 'We'll have the night, so, and the crew of the canoe will be waiting for us.'

'It's ever said that going to the King's house is not the same as coming from it,' said I, answering her.

'I suppose it's a long time since ye were here,' said Mrs. Long.

'There are forty-two years since I was here,' said I. 'I wasn't here since I married.'

She laughed.

'It's an unbelievable story,' she said.

'Yes, but it's true,' said I. 'On my soul I don't know where the chapel is at all, because there's a great change on this place since last I was here. I am like Rip since I came into this town. I don't recognize anybody and nobody recognizes me. But talk won't do us,' said I to Mary, 'come on and we'll look for the clerk. If he had everything ready we'd have no delay when the priest would come.'

'That's exactly what ye had better do,' said Mrs. Long, and we went out.

East with us to the chapel and as the luck of life would have it, the clerk was standing before us at the gate.

'God to ye, women of the island,' said he. 'I suppose it was the pension that brought ye this way?'

'It is, indeed,' said I.

'The devil, but I'm nearly out of my mind with the same pension since it was started. I don't like them, the old women, running in to me at all times,' said he.

'Musha, may God have mercy on us!' said I. 'Many a place there was one of them in hiding unknown to anybody until now. May God put no shake in the hand that invented it for them, because they are a long time burdened unknown to the world.'

'You are right in that much,' said the clerk. 'Come on into the chapel.'

We sat in on the seat and it wasn't long until he came with his armful of books and sat on the seat nearest to us.

'Yes,' said he, 'can ye give me any help? This is slow work. Let one of ye be praying while the other is answering me.'

'On my oath, I can't do any praying because I'm anxious, but maybe Mary could while I'd be answering. If the work were done first we would have plenty of time to pray then,' said I.

'Here's ye to it, then,' said he, and it took a good while of the day for him to do his job. When he had everything settled he left us there.

'Ye'll have to wait now until the priest comes,' said he.

Mary and I spent a nice short while in the chapel, but the priest came at last and it was a great relief to us.

When we came back to Mrs. Long she had a cup of tea ready before us, and to tell the truth I had need of it, because I didn't wait to eat anything in the morning.

'Ye'll be going home now, I suppose,' said she.

'We will,' said I, 'but we have decided to go to Harbour Town first to visit the sick woman. We'd have no business going home without paying her a visit.'

'Musha, you are right,' said she. 'Wasn't it fatal the way it happened to the poor woman? She is badly hurt.'

'Didn't you ever hear,' said I, 'that providence doesn't stop, and since the evening is fine, if we had the motor-car we'd pay a little visit down across.'

'On my soul, musha,' said she, 'it won't be that fine. The sky has the appearance of rain.'

I put my head out the door and the fine wide drops were falling down.

'It's raining already,' said I, 'and we have to go into Patrick Bowler's house yet. Farewell and bless you, woman of the house.'

We went out and the rain was falling heavily. Patrick was standing in the door before us and he chuckled.

'I think ye'll have Ballyferriter until morning, women of the island,' said he. 'It looks like it will do a good drenching of rain.'

'Yah! if we have itself,' said I, 'haven't you a long roomy house to give us lodging until morning?'

The weather lightened a little at last and we went to where the motor-car was, but we weren't a dozen yards from the house when the rain came, and the drop was in to the bone on us before we reached Mannion's house. A person would think we were two ducks with broken backs.

The Mannion had the motor-car ready to go to Dingle and he couldn't make much delay. He said he would bring us to Harbour Town, but that we'd have to stay there until morning. We had to put our minds at ease; we had no second choice.

When we got to the house the bright welcomes were before us. There was no thirst, hunger or cold left on us there or lack of entertainment either.

At ten o'clock in the morning the man of the motor-car was before us and while you'd be drinking a cup of tea we were at Cliff Top and the canoe had just come to meet us. The weather was not altogether too gentle and what with a fine blast of wind and sea-swells we were not too easy in our minds until we reached the Island.

But God of Power! After all the hardship and the length I had looked forward to the pension, I got no tale or tidings of it and I suppose it was the barren hope for me. It's hard on poor people to have anything, but as the man said long ago:

A person without store, at a wedding he's not recognized;
A person without store, his voice is not weighed in sense;
A person without store, he has no business spending or ordering;
And a person without store, is the butt of life's misfortune.

That's the same way with me and the pension. But I suppose Tim of Dingle is in the first place!

CHAPTER EIGHTEEN

The Last Chapter

My spell on this little bench is nearly finished. It's sad and low and lonely I am to be parting with it. Long as the day is, night comes, and alas, the night is coming for me, too.

I am parting with you, beautiful little place, sun of my life. Other people will have your pleasure in future, but I'll be far away from you in a kingdom I don't know. Big Peig, as the children call me, will be there no more, but maybe a better woman would. But she won't have as much pleasure as I had, because great as was my sorrow and heart-torment, God of Glory and His Blessed Mother helped me. I was often standing here studying the works of the Creator and tasting His royal sweetness in my heart. Everything He created was a consolation to me, even unto the grief itself, it would make me think deeper. I thought there was nothing in the things of this life but poverty—this place full today and empty tomorrow—hadn't I got it to be seen, clearly. The people I knew in my youth, it was often they had the stone in the gauntlet for each other. They were strong, courageous, strong-worded, but they all fell, they were cleared out of the world. It was the same do the people who were there before them got, and may God have mercy on us, where is their work today? Other people to be in their place, without the slightest thought for them. I think everything is folly except for loving God!

I am now at tight grips with the years, and many a thing I saw. Everything I was interested in I didn't let it astray. Someone else will have pastime out of my work when I'm gone on the way of truth. A person here and a person there will say, maybe, 'Who was that Peig Sayers?' but poor Peig will be the length of their shout from them. This green bench where she used to do the studying will be a domicile for the birds of the wilderness, and the little house where she used to eat and drink, it's unlikely there'll be a trace of it there.

These thoughts appearing in my heart today are lonely. They are not pleasant for me but I can't help them. Here they are towards me in their thousands; they are like soldiers. As I scatter them, they come together again. It's no good for me to be at them. They have beaten me. My blessing and the blessing of God be with Youth; and my advice to everyone is to borrow from this life, because a spool is no faster turning than it. My life is spent, as a candle, and my hope is up every day that I'll be called into the eternal kingdom.

O God who is in Heaven, my trust and my hope is fully in you! May you guide me on this long road I have not travelled before! It's often during my life you helped me. Well I know your holy help, because I was often held by sorrow, with no escape. When the need was highest, it was then you would lay your merciful eye on me, and a light like the shining of the sun would come on my worried mind. The clouds of sorrow would be gone without trace; in place there would be some spiritual joy whose sweetness I cannot describe here.

But I have this much to say, that I had good neighbours. We helped each other and lived in the shelter of each other. Everything that was coming dark upon us, we would disclose it to each other, and that would give us consolation of mind. Friendship was the fastest root in our hearts.

It was like a little rose in the wilderness I grew up; without for company only those gems that God of Glory created, eternal praise to Him! Every early morning in the summer when the sun would show its face up over the top of Eagle Mountain I was often looking at it and at the same time making wonder of the colours in the sky around us. I remember well that there used to be little yellow, golden rays as slender roads coming to me from the top of the mountain, and that the mountain used to be red and a big belt of every colour, between white, yellow and black, around the sky and every colour giving its own appearance on the great, wet sea. I think, there was welcome in the heart of every creature for the sparkling of the morning.

There are people and they think that this island is a lonely, airy place. That is true for them, but the peace of the Lord is in it. I am living in it for more than forty years, and I didn't see two of the neighbours fighting in it yet. It was like honey for my poor tormented heart to rise up on the shoulder of the mountain footing the turf or gathering the sods on each other. Very often I'd throw myself back in the green heather, resting. It wasn't for bone-laziness I'd do it, but for the beauty of the hills and the rumble of the waves that would be grieving down from me, in dark caves where the seals of the sea lived—those and the blue sky without a cloud travelling it, over me—it was those made me do it, because those were the pictures most pleasant to my heart, and it's those I was most used to.

A person would say, maybe, that it was a simple life we were living, but nobody would say that our life was comfortable. Our own hardships followed us. It's often we were in a way to go with fear and fright, because when winter came it wasn't its habit to come gentle and kind. The great sea was coming on top of us and the strong force of the wind helping it. We had but to send our prayer sincerely to God that nobody would be taken sick or ill. We had our own charge of that because there wasn't a priest or doctor near us without going across the little strait and the little strait was up to three miles in length. But God was in favour with us, eternal praise to Him! For with my memory nobody died without the priest in winter-time.

Farewell to the things of this life now, and especially to the pleasant, gay time I have spent here. I'm afraid I'll do no more work in future for the language of the superior men, but I have done a person's share, maybe. I would do as much more, and have the heart for it, but the time is spent.

Pray for me, friends and dear people, that God will give me help for the long road!

THE BLASKET GROUP
and
contiguous mainland.

Syb

F

Clogher H

Carrig Valach

Inish
Túiscirt

Beg-ini
Blasket
Sound

Great
Blasket

Village

Tearacht

Great Sound

Inish-
na-Bró

Narrow Sound

Inish-vickillaun

Thunder
Rock

Foze
Rocks

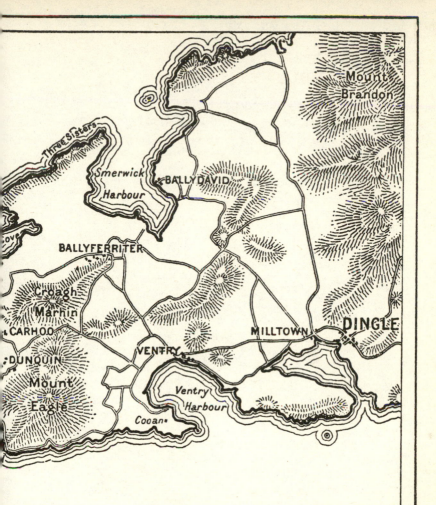

Mount
Brandon

Three Sisters

Smerwick
Harbour

BALLYDAVID

ove

BALLYFERRITER

Croagh
Marhin

CARHOO

DUNQUIN

Mount
Eagle

VENTRY

Ventry
Harbour

Cooan

MILLTOWN

DINGLE

BAY OF DINGLE

k

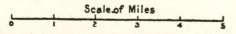

Dingle to Tralee, 31 miles.
Dingle to Dublin, 238 miles.

Scale of Miles

0   1   2   3   4   5